CAVOUR

CAVOUR.

CAVOUR

by

MAURICE PALÉOLOGUE

Formerly Ambassador at the Court of
St. Petersburg

Translated
by Ian F. D. Morrow and
Muriel M. Morrow

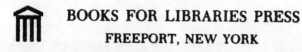
BOOKS FOR LIBRARIES PRESS
FREEPORT, NEW YORK

First Published 1927
Reprinted 1970

92
C 383 p

MN

INTERNATIONAL STANDARD BOOK NUMBER:
0-8369-5534-X

LIBRARY OF CONGRESS CATALOG CARD NUMBER:
77-130561

PRINTED IN THE UNITED STATES OF AMERICA

TRANSLATOR'S INTRODUCTION

"GREAT men owe a fourth part of their fame to their daring," wrote the Italian poet and dramatist, Ugo Foscolo, who died in the year that Cavour was gazetted a Lieutenant in the Royal Engineers at Turin, " two-fourths to fortune, and the remaining fourth to their crimes." His saying aptly sums up the life-work of Cavour. The great " architect " of United Italy was a singular compound of daring with astuteness; of Machiavellian realism with Liberal idealism; of hot passions with an almost inhuman coldness of intellect. Behind all these qualities, fusing them into a living and sparkling entity, lay the animating and dominating trait in Cavour's many-sided character—patriotism. " It belongs to great men "—runs the old French proverb—" to have great defects "; and it would be idle to pretend that Cavour was any exception to this rule. Alike in his private and public life there is much that the moralist is constrained to condemn. When, however, all has been said that can be said in the way of derogation, an unassailable quality in the man remains : his transcendent ability.

Although he died nearly seventy years ago, Cavour has had long to wait for his biographer. From time to time biographies have been published in different languages, and of very varying degrees of merit. With one exception, and that a work written primarily for the scholar and professional

5

historian, the present volume is the first in which an attempt
has been made to portray the lineaments of the man as well
as the statesman. M. Paléologue's eminent qualifications
for undertaking such a task do not need to be explained
to a public already well acquainted with an accomplished
memoirist and historian. His lifelong experience in diplomacy
gives a peculiar authority to his account of Cavour's foreign
policy. Nor does Cavour himself require any introduction
to English-speaking readers whose ancestors contributed so
largely to that enfranchisement of Italy for which Cavour
worked and fought with all his heart and soul and intellect.

Happy in his life, and in the knowledge, which was his
before he died, that his life-work was about to be crowned
with success, Cavour was no less happy in the moment of
his death. For he died at fifty-one, before Age had come
to dull the brilliant intellect, or enfeeble the vigorous physique,
and yet, in Lord Palmerston's memorable phrase, not " too
soon for his glory or his fame." In the hierarchy of European statesmen his name stands out with a quite peculiar
distinction, for to him was given what is granted to very
few men—to be the creator of a nation, the " architect " of
a great modern State.

IAN F. D. MORROW.

AUTHOR'S PREFACE

IN 19— a Prince of an Imperial House then ruling in Europe paid a State visit to Victor Emmanuel III. On the conclusion of the formal ceremonies the King offered to conduct his guest through Rome in order that he might show him what travellers in olden days called the *mirabilia urbis Romæ*. The offer was accepted, and the King and the Prince at once set out under the heavenly sky of a Roman spring.

But the Prince, who was devoid of intelligence and still more of knowledge, took not the slightest interest in the well-informed explanations proffered by his Royal guide. He displayed the most complete indifference to the celebrated remains of pagan and Christian Rome—to the Seven Columns, the Forum, the triumphal arches, the basilicas and palaces, and even to the Coliseum. His mind was occupied exclusively with thoughts of pleasures of a different order with which he intended to pass the evening.

As the carriage passed along the Prati di Castello, the Prince noticed a large building. Over the door was written : *Caserne Cavour*. "What does 'Cavour' mean ? " he inquired. But without waiting for an answer he exclaimed : " I know. It must be the name of the architect." " You are right," replied Victor Emmanuel III. " He was an architect ; a famous architect ; it was he who built Italy."

By these words the grandson of the first King of Italy not only paid a grateful tribute to his grandfather's great minister, but bore Royal witness to the essential truth of a great historical fact. The architect of United Italy was, in truth, one of those statesmen who have impressed their personality very deeply on the destinies of their country and their age—one of those who have shown themselves the most startling exceptions to Tolstoy's brilliant paradox, by revealing in everything they undertook in the realm of politics a rapid and lucid intellect, a balanced reason, and a powerful and steadfast purpose.

It is from this standpoint that the following portrait of Cavour has been painted. A rough sketch—nothing more —in which it is sought to delineate the most original and individual traits in this remarkable character, to reveal the inner man, to lay bare the sources of his inspiration, the mental processes by which he came to his decisions, and the manner in which he worked.

CONTENTS

CHAPTER I

THE DAYS OF YOUTH

ATAVISM of Cavour. His precociousness: "Our son is very original."—The Military Academy at Turin; a page to the King.—Garrison life in the Alps. Genoa; his first impressions of the ducal city.—Revolution of 1830. Exile at Fort Bard. Cavour resigns his commission.—His life as a country gentleman. His quick intellect, realism, decisiveness, and boldness in experiment: the chief qualities that later characterised the statesman.—Passion for politics. Visit to Paris and to London in 1835. Friendship with Tocqueville; comparison of their minds.—Regretful return to country life; Léri.—Cavour and women. His amorousness; his keen psychological intuition; his capacity for seizing an opportunity. *L'Incognita*; likeness to Mirabeau. —Cavour's busy life at Léri; splendid results obtained from his agricultural experiments.—His clear grasp of great economic problems. The railway problem leads Cavour to the conception of Italian unity . . . pp. 25–59

CHAPTER II

THE FIRST ADVENTURE

CHAPTER III

CAVOUR AND THE SPHINX

CHAPTER IV

ORSINI

Mazzini, Pallavicino, La Farina, Garibaldi. The Italian Nationalist Society under the direction of Cavour is the most efficient factor in promoting revolt.—Aggressive attitude of Piedmontese diplomacy towards Austria. Cavour's skilful aggressiveness: " If it comes to the point we shall show ourselves refractory children."—What was passing in the mind of the Sphinx in the Tuileries ?—Cavour's agents in Paris: Dr. Conneau, Mme Cornu, Alexander Bixio. The mission of the Countess Castiglione: " Succeed, my cousin, by whatever means you please; but succeed ! " The Florentine Judas.—Napoleon's enigmatic mind: *Cæsar Imperator*. Grave doubts inspired in the Emperor's counsellors by the new turn given to French policy. His nebulous ideas; his cloudy mysticism; he is hypnotised by the contemplation of far horizons.—The tragic night of 14 January 1858. Orsini. The trial; Jules Favre's speech; Orsini's letter to the Emperor: " Unless Italy is free the peace of Your Majesty and of the rest of Europe will be no more than an illusion. . . ." The verdict. Orsini's second letter to the Emperor; his last wishes. On the scaffold: " Long live Italy ! "—Orsini's letters drafted by Jules Favre inspired by Napoleon III; secret negotiations with the Prefect of Police, Piétri, with Orsini.—Strong impression made on the Emperor by Orsini's attempt. His personal bravery unquestioned; but he fears for the future of his throne and his dynasty: the weakness of the Imperial regime beneath its imposing exterior. Believing the Italians to be irrevocably determined to assassinate him, Napoleon III realises the enfranchisement of Italy has become of vital necessity to him.

CHAPTER V

THE INTERVIEW AT PLOMBIÈRES

LEARNING of Orsini's attempt of 14 January, Cavour exclaimed: " Good God! let us hope they are not Italians! "—The reactionary passions set loose in France compel the Imperial Government to demand that Piedmont should take measures against conspirators. Virulent language of Walewski; tension in diplomatic relations between Paris and Turin; dexterity shown by Cavour in this crisis.—A dramatic stroke. Napoleon III secretly sends Cavour Orsini's letters with a request to publish them in the Official Gazette.—The Emperor once more fascinated by his Italian dream. He conceives of his mission as one conferred upon him by Providence: the age of the Antonines and the Napoleonic peace. Great illusions. An idealist who believes himself a man of action. Drouyn de Lhuys's cruel saying: " The Emperor is endowed with immense desires and limited capacities; he seeks to achieve extraordinary things and he accomplishes only extravagant ones."—Dr. Conneau's secret visit to Turin. Napoleon III invites Cavour to Plombières on 21 July to speak privately with him.—Cavour's mysterious journey; false passport. The interview between the two conspirators: a scene worthy of Shakespeare. By what device could Austria be brought to declare war? What should be done when victory had been won? The Emperor's ideas upon the political and territorial organisation of the Peninsula; his plan for an Italian Confederation over which the Pope should preside. The eventual

CHAPTER VI

THE MARRIAGE OF PRINCESS CLOTILDA WITH PRINCE NAPOLEON

VICTOR EMMANUEL receives with enthusiasm the stipulations of Plombières: "To gain our ends, guns are necessary, and as soon as possible." The idea of marrying his daughter to Prince Napoleon lessens his joy. Cavour points out to him the political necessity for this marriage.—The great rôle which Victor Emmanuel is to play henceforth in the *Risorgimento*; his good qualities as a king; comparison with Henri IV.—Cavour sets to work immediately to develop the military resources of Piedmont and to prepare for the events which are to oblige Austria to take up arms. His prodigious activity.—He sends his most intimate confidant to Paris, Chevalier Nigra, in order to have better control over his secret agents.—Napoleon III admirably conceals his policy from Europe; peaceful speech at Cherbourg; pilgrimage to Sainte-Anne d'Auray; Walewski congratulates himself on the wise lines along which the Emperor is moving.—The mission of Prince Napoleon to Warsaw; a new phase opened in the conspiracy which is developing between Paris and Turin.—Elaboration of the

CHAPTER VII

SOLFERINO AND VILLAFRANCA

WHILE the King takes command of the Piedmontese army Cavour unites in his own hand the political, financial, and administrative organisations for national defence.—Revolutions at Modena, Parma, Bologna, and Florence. Installation of Piedmontese Commissioners. Rising of the Marches and Umbria.—Arrival of Napoleon III at Genoa. His delirious reception; a day of apotheosis and wild excitement. His proclamation to the Army of Italy: " The Sacred Way."—General offensive by the Allies. Victory of Magenta on 4 June; entry into Milan on 8 June; victory of Solferino on 24 June. Sudden cessation of the offensive; undisturbed retreat of the Austrians behind the Adige.— General Fleury's mission to Verona. Napoleon III offers an armistice to Francis Joseph, who accepts it.—Conclusion of armistice astonishes Cavour. He leaves at once for the Royal headquarters at Monzambano on the Mincio. He earnestly begs Victor Emmanuel not to sign a premature peace; their violent quarrel. Greatly enraged, Cavour

CHAPTER VIII

THE STATESMAN AND THE *CONDOTTIERE*

CHAPTER IX

FROM VICTORY TO DEATH

COMPLEXITY of the task imposed upon Cavour ; change of method.—The Venetian question ; all solutions are laid aside ; but the imprescriptible rights of *Italia irredenta* are solemnly affirmed before Europe.—The Roman Question ; secret negotiations with the Holy See in order to obtain the voluntary renunciation by the Pope of his political and temporal sovereignty ; favourable progress of the negotiations ; sudden *volte-face* by the Vatican.   Cavour at once returns to the problem in endeavouring to come to an agreement with Napoleon III to withdraw his troops from Rome.— Internal organisation of the new Italy ; the spirit of Liberalism inspiring Cavour.—The Garibaldi scandal ; tragic sitting of Italian Chamber on 18 April 1861.—Cavour exhausted : attacked by the deadly marsh-fever ; its rapid progress. Cavour's confession *in extremis* ; Father Giacomo and his penitent excommunicant.   The confessor hailed before the Holy Office.   The last moments of Cavour ; his death on 6 June 1861 .   .   .   .   .   .   pp. 279–294

ILLUSTRATIONS

CHAPTER I

THE DAYS OF YOUTH

CHAPTER I

THE DAYS OF YOUTH

CAMILLE DE CAVOUR was born in Turin on 10 August 1810, and was descended from an old Piedmontese family the Benso, which, in the reign of Frederick Barbarossa, had won renown in the Third Crusade. Through his paternal grandmother, Philippine de Sales, he was related to the Savoyard nobility; and to a brother of the saintly bishop Francis de Sales. On the side of his Genevan and Protestant mother, Adèle de Sellon, he sprang from an old Huguenot house of Languedoc; while in the persons of his maternal aunts, Baronne d'Auzers and the Duchesse de Clermont-Tonnerre, who had made the Palazzo Cavour in Turin their home, the ties formerly uniting his ancestors with the French aristocracy were in a measure renewed.

It was in Turin, the capital of Piedmont, that Cavour first saw the light of day; and it was in that city, or in the Piedmontese countryside, that he passed his whole life. Seldom did he cross the frontiers of Piedmont, and then only to visit Geneva or Paris or London. Only once did Cavour visit Florence. And the creator of United Italy never saw with his own eyes Parma or Bologna, Venice or Rome or Naples. Thus it is not surprising that in later days his enemies should have reviled his " Piedmontism," and even accused him of wishing to " Piedmontise " Italy. Later

25

on it will be necessary to examine more closely the grounds on which this accusation was based.

In the course of centuries many foreign branches had been grafted on to the Italian stem of Cavour's family tree. But Cavour was none the less an Italian because foreign blood ran in his veins; he was, on the contrary, an Italian to the very core of his being. What he derived from the mingling of racial strains within him was an ability to look upon his native land, and all things Italian, with a certain degree of objectivity. Raised by virtue of his mingled ancestry above merely national and regional, feelings and ideas, Cavour was rendered capable of a deeper understanding, a clearer and more synthetic vision, of the national soul and genius of Italy.

The traits displayed by Cavour in his earliest childhood revealed the manner of man he was to become. In his mother's eyes he was " a jolly boy, strong and noisy, and always playing "—to keep him quiet was an impossibility. With tireless energy he ran up and down the big family mansion; he slammed doors; and twenty times a day he visited his adoring aunts. On his father's vast country estate at Santéna young Camille romped and played like a frisky colt. Filled with animal spirits, he was endowed as well with a healthy constitution and dynamic energy. His grandmother and mother—both women of character and ability—were his teachers in reading, writing, and arithmetic; but he was a poor pupil. He hated work; he idled; he slept over his books; he stared at the ceiling. At the age of five, in the first of his writings that has come down to us, he wrote : " Study bores me. What can I do ? It is not my fault." Who could have foreseen that this unwilling learner would become in later life a glutton for work, taking upon his own shoulders the cares of half a dozen ministries, and working all his colleagues to death ? Yet the explanation is a simple one. A child rarely sees in the alphabet, or in numbers, any real meaning ; and Cavour was never interested except in realities or—to be more exact —in concrete realities. His dislike throughout life for " bureaucratic red-tapeism " witnesses to this truth. Neither books nor documents, calculations nor statistics, had any value in his sight except as the indispensable means to action ; as an arsenal of practical arguments ; as a preamble as tedious as necessary, which should for that reason be as concise as possible.

But when he was twelve a change became apparent. He displayed a sudden passion for work ; a sudden bursting-forth of intellectual activity ; a hunger for reading. Nevertheless his physical desires and activities remained unaltered. His father, the Marquis Cavour, in a letter to his wife depicts this spontaneous outburst of their son's childish faculties. " Our son is very original," wrote the Marquis. " First he dines very well off a large bowl of soup, two fine cutlets, some boiled beef, a snipe which I brought him from the rice-fields, rice, potatoes and haricot beans, some grapes, and then coffee ; he cannot be induced to eat anything else. After dinner, he recites to me verses from Dante, the sonnets of Petrarch, and passages from the writings of Corticelli, Alfieri, Filicaïa, and Jacopo Ortis, striding up and down in a dressing-gown with his hands in his pockets." Is it only fancy, or does one catch a glimpse of another hand writing of " the deeds and prowesses of Pantagruel in his infancy that made his father to rejoice by a natural affection " ?

With his entry into the Military College at Turin, where young nobles were taught the profession of arms, Cavour was at once subjected to a rigorous training and discipline. From the first his acute intelligence was attracted by mathematics and geography as favourite subjects of study ; but the confined and disciplined life irked him dreadfully. He showed himself disobedient, not through caprice or baseness, but under the urge of an instinct already well developed within him.   When given an order, however pleasantly, he flushed and became very angry.   On more than one occasion he was placed under arrest " for insolent replies."   Despite this behaviour, his father's influence at Court procured him the post of page to the Heir Apparent, the Prince of Carignan, who was soon to ascend the throne as Charles Albert ; and Cavour attended Court functions arrayed in a purple coat embroidered with gold lace.   But he very soon wearied of a life of pomp and formal ceremonies, and he hated the feeling of servility that some of his duties aroused in him. At times he was disrespectful and mocking, and—worst fault of all—he gave vent to his liberal opinions.   These indiscretions were brought to the notice of the Prince of Carignan ; and the storm broke.   " Camille de Cavour," wrote the Prince, " is a little Radical. I have shown him the door."   Tears and lamentations in the Cavour family ! But the young rebel himself was overjoyed, looking upon his disgrace as a deliverance from slavery. It was ended—this " life of a

lackey ! " No longer would he be compelled to wear a
" lobster's coat ! "

On 17 September 1826, at the age of sixteen, he passed
brilliantly the final examinations in the Military College, and
was gazetted as a lieutenant to the Royal Engineers stationed
at Turin. At home in the old Cavour palace once more, he
was obliged to veil his liberal sympathies, for in all Piedmont
there was to be found none more faithful to the Throne and
the Altar, none more submissive to the Congregation, than
his father, the Marquis Cavour. But that mattered very
little to the boy. His two aunts, Mmes d'Auzers and de
Clermont-Tonnerre, both childless, adored him. They were
clever, tender, full of vivacity, and surrounded by an atmosphere of charm ; and he owed to them that agile wit,
that ease of manner, that facility in sparkling conversation,
that were to be of the greatest service to him in later life.
Another, and no less important, influence in the development
of his character was a visit he paid to his uncle, Comte de
Sellon, at Geneva. There Jean Jacques Rousseau, Voltaire,
Gibbon, Mme de Staël, Benjamin Constant, Schlegel, and
Sismondi were still held in remembrance, and around the
shores of Lake Leman the fragrance of the eighteenth century
still lingered. Comte de Sellon was steeped in those memories.
A disciple of Turgot and Condorcet—philanthropist and
economist—he firmly believed in the steady progress of the
human race along the paths of Reason and Liberty. Many
and intimate were the conversations between uncle and
nephew, and Cavour gained from them a clearer and more
profound understanding of liberal principles for the promotion of the betterment of mankind. He always remembered

with gratitude this time of moral expansion, and ever afterwards spoke with deep feeling of the " life-giving air of
Switzerland." But the profession of arms has its duties
and, as Vigny says, its thraldom. By the treaties of 1815
Sardinia had been compelled to fortify its Alpine frontier
against renewed aggression on the part of France. So
greatly had Napoleon's brilliant campaigns impressed the
Austrian General Staff, so fearful were they still of terrifying
surprises like Albenga, Montenotte, and Marengo, that their
eyes were continually turned towards the height of Tende
and the valleys of Susa and Aosta. Under the harsh and
captious supervision of Metternich, the Piedmontese Government carried out the fortification of the entire Alpine
frontier.

In August 1828 Cavour was ordered to Ventimiglia, where
the engineers were erecting a line of forts to guard the Roya
Valley and the Corniche Road. It was a miserable country-
side. There was no society of any kind, and when not
engaged on his military duties Cavour, as his sole means of
recreation, took long and solitary walks, or buried himself
in his beloved books. In this quiescence he began to know
himself, to form ideas, and to quicken his perceptions. A
letter to his brother, written on 30 November 1828, shows
already in their full development those three qualities that
ruled and conditioned all the others, and that afterwards
served him so well in his political career—independence of
character, strength of conviction, and stubborn vigour. " My
family accuse me of betraying my name," he wrote, " my
country, and my caste. Heaven is my witness that I would
rather end my days a prisoner than commit an act unworthy

of my name, or of the dignity of a free man. Personal considerations, and the probable advantages from a political and material point of view, beckon me to enlist under the banner of absolutism. But an innate regard for my moral dignity has always prevented me from entering upon a life in which I should have to abandon my convictions and not believe in anything that was not the belief of those around me."

Some months later, in the middle of winter, he was transferred from the temperate climate of the Corniche to the snow-clad neighbourhood of Mont Cenis, where he assisted in fortifying Exilles on the bank of the Doire and Esseillon in the Valley of the Arc. No less desolate than the Ligurian Alps, this district was far more impressive in its austere magnificence; and it gave, as it were, an electric shock to Cavour's entire nature. He indulged in a perfect frenzy of work; but a frenzy that persisted and was controlled by a system with which no amusements were permitted to interfere. As he wrote to the Comte de Sellon, the uncle who had become the receptacle of his confidences: " I study mathematics and mechanics, as for these I have the most aptitude. I also think that a knowledge of history and modern languages is very useful. But it seems to me that if one desires to become famous one must learn to concentrate. The rays of the sun when brought together by a lens can set fire to a wood upon which, individually, they can produce no effect." A first result of his serious studies was an emancipation from the religious faith of his fathers. The religious beliefs which had been inculcated in him in infancy, which had inspired up to the present his moral life, were almost entirely dissipated without any severe internal struggle or any sacrifice, through the quiet influence of exact reason and at the imperious command of knowledge and of the desire to be true to himself. For Catholicism, however, and above all for its ritual, he continued to have a respectful sympathy that almost amounted to affection—*ripæ ulterioris amore.* The great ecclesiastical reform of 1855—one of the most important acts in his career—his lofty conception of " a free Church in a free State," had already begun to germinate in his mind.

Another attribute was brought to the surface by the daily hours of study—his political ability. He suddenly received a presentiment of the part awaiting him on the stage of history. " If I thought," he wrote to de Sellon, on 28 June 1828, " that one day, however distant, I could render useful service in public life without having to abandon my convictions, I would willingly give up these dry studies and wearying calculations in order to devote myself eagerly to another kind of work." But was that possible? Could he enter public life without the sacrifice of his convictions? That stupid monarch Charles Felix—a dull fellow with ever-open mouth and slobbering lips—was completely under the thumb of the Jesuits. In his thick head one idea reigned—theocratic absolutism. And, in defence of his belief, he was capable of the most atrocious cruelties without respect for justice, rank, or personal worth. After the disturbances in 1821, it was commonly said in Turin, " every noble family will soon count its dead." The police were omnipotent, seizing, at the frontiers, newspapers and books. Within the country they suppressed all freedom of thought.

Their spies were everywhere and no home was safe or sacred. Under such a regime that " young Jacobin " Cavour could scarce conceive of entering public life ; and indeed it is to his credit that he was incapable of doing so. No vulgar ambition, no desire for power at any cost, possessed him. He was incapable of saying with Julien Sorel in *Rouge et Noir* : " In the time of Napoleon it was the thing to be a soldier ; one could become a general at thirty-six. But now it is the priests who hold sway. I will therefore become a priest and sell the faithful a seat in Heaven." Cavour could never sacrifice to the idols of the day. When in power, he pursued a single aim and sought to gratify a single desire : the application of his ideals in the government of his country. Yet, as he wandered lost in meditation over the snow-clad slopes of Mount Cenis, a vision that remained with him throughout life gradually took shape before his eyes : the vision of an " unhappy Italy bowed down under the weight of a religious and civil despotism." In a letter to a young English friend he wrote : " Have pity on those who, their souls animated by the generous ideal of modern civilisation, yet see their native land oppressed by Austrian bayonets. Tell your countrymen that Italy is not unworthy of liberty because some of her sons are corrupt. Forgive me that I pour out my sad and angry heart to you." " Unhappy Italy "—for the first time we encounter the name of Italy in the handwriting of Cavour.

In May 1830 he was transferred to Genoa. After his rough life in the Alps, this beautiful city provoked a sudden expansion of all his faculties and intoxicated him with joy. His cousin de La Rive, who knew him intimately, has left

an admirable description of him as he was at this time:
" How could Genoa, that brilliant and beautiful city of the
South, wealthy, hospitable, bathed in sunshine, a city of
light and life, of action and affairs no less than of ideas, fail
to fascinate and enchant a young man full of vigour and
fire, ardent, athirst for action and liberty, who had known
only the inclement skies and sultry atmosphere of Turin ?
On the other hand, it is not surprising that the wit and
vivacity, the natural grace of manner, of Camille de Cavour
opened all doors to him and conquered all hearts.   In Genoa
he first took his place in the world, and I have heard it said
that this great school of statecraft could add nothing to his
accomplishments."   The ancient ducal republic, proud birthplace of Doria and Fieschi, of Spinola and Grimaldi, guarded
jealously the traditions of pride and liberty that animated its
oldest families.   On 30 and 31 July 1830 the city was raised
to the highest pitch of excitement by the news of the Revolution in Paris, the flight of Charles X, the exile of the Bourbons,
and the advent of a constitutional monarchy.   Hope suddenly
filled all hearts, for now that France had become the leader
of the liberal movement the hour of freedom had struck for
the nations.   As for Cavour, he was intoxicated with
enthusiasm and joy.   Already he beheld " Italy wrested from
the shameful rule of Austrian bayonets and Papal excom-
munications."   Henceforth men would be free to think—
" one would be able to speak aloud."   Noble ideals and
generous aspirations would no longer be suppressed " as a
crime against the State, or as sacrilege."   But his rejoicing
was short-lived ; the time had not yet come for " speaking
aloud."   His daring words were brought to the knowledge

of the military authorities, and he was accused of sedition and of having cried " Long live Louis Philippe." He was even suspected of being a member of the Carbonari. King Charles Felix was not the man to treat such conduct as mere high spirits. One fine morning Lieutenant Cavour awoke to find that he had been ordered to proceed forthwith to Bard in the Valley of the Aosta to superintend the work of masons who were engaged in erecting a fort. This fort was built on so steep a rock, in a wild pass so narrow, and with walls so precipitous, that the River Doire could scarcely force its way through. There an Austrian battalion for eight days in May 1800 had prevented the French army from descending from the St. Bernard Pass. The future of Bonaparte came nigh to being shattered against that rock ; and it was there that Marengo was won. It played as decisive a part in Cavour's career. Without a friend, withdrawn from the world, he lived for nine months a dreary penance in which his sole relaxation was a game of picquet with the overseer of the works. Far from dispiriting him, this trial inspired him to one of those decisive and irremissible resolutions which are taken only by strong characters. On 12 November 1831 he resigned his commission.

II

It, indeed, required courage on his part to forsake a military career. As a younger son, he had no fortune of his own ; and " his dreadful reputation for entertaining liberal opinions " excluded him from any administrative post. But his parents, his elder brother Gustave, and his aunts Mmes d'Auzers and de Clermont-Tonnerre, were all too fond of him to abandon him to his fate. His whole family, although disapproving " his political heresies," exerted themselves on his behalf. The Marquis Cavour had inherited vast estates scattered over Piedmont ; at Grinzane, on the northern slopes of the Apennines ; at Santéna, in the vineyards of Montferrat ; at Léri, near Verceil, between the Po and the Sésia. At Grinzane Camille now made his home, occupying himself in the administration of the estate. At first he could not reconcile himself to this change in his life with its resultant sacrifices. Plunged in gloomy thought, he told and re-told the tale of all he had renounced ; he measured the depth of his fall. Writing to the Marchioness Giulia Barolo, a friend of his parents to whom he had always been much attached, he poured out his heart : " Is it surprising that when young, high-spirited, proud, and early thrown into contact with the world and politics, one should be ambitious, and desirous of fame and glory ? I confess to you there was a time when *I should have thought it quite natural to wake up one fine morning Prime Minister of the Kingdom of Italy !* " At the time when he penned this strange confession amounting almost to a presentiment, he was only twenty-two years old. But his courage soon gained the upper hand, and unavailing regrets ceased to trouble him. In this fact is to be found exemplified one of the predominant traits in his personality : the ability to apply himself with great concentration to whatever task he had in hand, and to grapple passionately with the realities of life. Once he had overcome the monotony of an agriculturist's existence, he began to find an " unexpected charm " in sowing a field of potatoes, planting vines, draining a meadow, raising fine cattle, and even in " turning over the manure-heap."

His cousin La Rive has left us yet another characteristic portrait of him—this time as a gentleman farmer " rising at dawn, inspecting his stables, seeing that each workman had his appointed task, overseeing their labours under a broiling sun, never content with giving a general direction but invariably concerning himself with the smallest details of the work, keeping a watchful eye on all mechanical inventions and fresh discoveries in chemistry that might be of service to him; continually experimenting and testing the results of his experiments with care and common sense, abandoning one experiment and repeating others on a scale which aston-ished the good neighbours who came anxiously seeking his advice. And always he was gay and affable, giving to each comer good counsel and encouragement concealed in some witty observation." Under this guise of gentleman farmer may be seen the statesman with his keen intelligence, his broad outlook, his decision, his initiative, his bold invention always restrained within the bounds of the possible, his good-humour, accessibility, and that gift of instinctive sympathy which is so invaluable in handling men.

Nevertheless politics remained the secret and dominant passion of his life. An unhappy passion, in that what he saw happening around him wounded him to the heart. Nothing remained of the high hopes that had been founded on the July Revolution; the tide of liberal ideas was im-prisoned within the frontiers of France; and the hand of Metternich once again hurled an unhappy Italy " into her century-old degradation." The new King of Piedmont,

Charles Albert, was no less miserable than his predecessor, the stupid Charles Felix. Cavour, indeed, felt towards the monarch to whom he had once been page a sort of physical aversion, an almost unconquerable repugnance. The personality of the one was in such entire opposition to that of the other as to render impossible any sort of relationship between the two. That of Charles Albert was so elusive that even his intimates failed to comprehend him. Unusually tall, with a high forehead and expressionless eyes, he was always morose, taciturn, and evasive; at times filled with sadness, ridden by fear, inspired by gloomy forebodings and remorse. Although by temperament ascetic and superstitiously religious, he was unable to live without feminine society; and he loved women with a queer mysticism in which " the fragrance of myrrh and incense mingled with that of powder *à la maréchale.*" In his political ideas there is to be found the same bizarre contrast. Animated to the depths of his being by a belief in the principle of Divine Right, he was nevertheless embroiled in 1821 in a liberal affray. Later he repented of his action, and in order to ease his conscience he fought against the Spanish Liberals at Cadiz under the command of the Duc d'Angoulême. But even this penitential crusade did not suffice to wash away the stain of his misconduct. Having caught the malaria of revolution, he ever afterwards carried the germ in his veins like a subtle poison that at times caused him to shiver as with an ague. Then there were those unceasing conflicts in his inner self; that vacillating, disconcerting, paradoxical appearance; that likeness to Hamlet and the Sphinx which caused one of his servitors to say of him: " His looks invariably belie his words ; his words contradict his smile ; his smile veils his thoughts." And one day he himself let fall from his bloodless lips the terrible avowal : " I am never sure of myself either in love or in politics." Obviously there could be no common meeting-ground for this ill-balanced, neurasthenic, fantastic monarch and the healthy and common-sense agriculturist of Grinzane.

But about this time a new influence entered into Cavour's life. Since Louis Philippe had ascended the throne, France had been represented at Turin by Baron Prosper de Barante. A man of the world, clever, cultured, this former friend of Madame de Staël, this privileged confidant of the Duchesse de Dino, had for secretaries two young men, the Comtes de Sesmaisons and d'Haussonville, who were ardent supporters of the liberal cause. The French Legation had become the rendezvous and, as it were, the headquarters of the Liberal Party in Piedmont. Whenever he could escape from Léri, Cavour never failed to put in an appearance at the Legation. There he met the chivalrous and charming Marquis d'Azeglio, the poet Silvio Pellico, and the warm-hearted Count Balbo. But, above all, it was the ambassador whom he came to see and to interrogate. After the ambassador it was the secretaries' turn. Comte d'Haussonville has left a record of their interminable talks. " It was no light task to explain to the future Prime Minister of the Italy of 1859 all that he desired to know about men and affairs in the France of 1830. Once embarked on this topic, conversation went on for hours. Occasionally, with the avidity and self-confidence of youth, we passed an entire night in this manner. I lauded the merits of our parliamentary institutions, while he dreamed of

the day when he would give them to his own country!"
But the best way in which to understand "men and affairs
in the France of 1830" was to observe them upon the spot.
In February 1835 Cavour left for Paris, where he stayed
until the beginning of May.

The mental exhilaration which he had experienced five
years before at Genoa he felt even more strongly in the
atmosphere of Paris. Moreover, he had the good fortune
to witness a ministerial crisis of the first magnitude. The
Cabinet over which Marshal Mortier, Duc de Trévise,
presided, had resigned. The early days of the succeeding
Cabinet were full of troubles and within three weeks it had
fallen. Then the Duc de Broglie was successful in forming
a Government with the aid of Thiers and Guizot. This
lengthy parliamentary episode filled with crises, with secret
intrigues and combinations, with personal rivalries and selfish
calculations, seemed to Cavour the most instructive and
engaging of spectacles: the natural and proper working of
constitutional government. Moreover he was in a position
to view it at close quarters.

The introductions with which he had been armed by
Barante opened to him the doors of the most exclusive
salons. Keenly observant, and with all his faculties on the
alert, Cavour was constantly to be seen in the *salons* of
Mmes de Castellane, de Boigne, de Circourt, of the Duchesse
de Rohan, the Princesse Belgiojoso, and of Mme Swetchine;
and he lent an attentive ear to the words of the protagonists
in the parliamentary combat of the day—the Duc de Broglie,
Marshal Soult, Molé, Guizot, Thiers, Duchâtel, the Chan-
cellor Pasquier, etc. etc. From all the brilliant talk to which

GUIZOT.

he listened he gained so strong an impression of the indestructible character of modern democracy that it became one
of his political axioms. Writing on 31 March 1835 to his
cousin La Rive, he said : " We can no longer deceive ourselves : Society is moving fast towards democracy. It is
impossible to forecast the form that it will take. But funda-
mentally it cannot be doubted that the reconstruction of
aristocratic government as such is impossible. Aristocracy
is falling to pieces, and the princes no less than the common
people are destroying it ; the patriciate has no longer a place
in modern political life. What then is left as a barrier against
the popular flood ? Nothing solid, nothing strong, nothing
durable. Is this for good or evil ? I do not know. But
in my opinion it is the inevitable goal of humanity. Let us
then prepare ourselves, or at least prepare our sons, that they
may give it greater consideration than we have done."

Soon an unexpected opportunity in which to study the
problem in all its aspects came to him. Desirous of continuing and extending his political and social studies, Cavour
left Paris for London on 3 May 1835 ; and it was his good
fortune to have as fellow-traveller Alexis de Tocqueville,
who at that moment had published the early chapters of his
Democracy in America. The two young men of almost equal
age (Cavour was five years the younger) were well suited to
one another. Both were interested in the brilliant spectacle
of English society ; they discussed the Reform Bill, the ecclesiastical laws, the Irish problem, pauperism, education,
prison reform, the Labour question, etc. etc. ; above all, the
great actors on the parliamentary stage—the Duke of Welling-
ton, Lords Grey, Melbourne, and Palmerston, Sir Robert

Peel, and Daniel O'Connell. Thus they laid the foundations of a great friendship. And, indeed, they were born to understand and delight one another. Alike in age, they belonged to the same social order and spoke the same language; they were alike in being highly gifted intellectually and emotionally, in their ardent patriotism, in their regard for the glory and welfare of their respective countries, in their common desire to pursue a public career, and in their common faith in the tonic virtue of liberal institutions. There, however, their resemblance to one another ended; and perhaps nothing affords a better understanding of Cavour's creative genius than a consideration of those qualities that distinguished Tocqueville from him.

The author of *Democracy in America* was pre-eminently a doctrinaire; he believed that reason alone could and should govern human affairs. He reduced all politics to rational ideas, and to a sort of systematised philosophy which held all the unforeseen contingencies, the unaccountable incidents, the blind forces of regal Destiny, and (as Frederick the Great expressed it) "the caprices of His Majesty King Hazard," to be as negligible and insignificant as the illogical dynamism of individual and collective passion, the ambitions, dreams of glory, illusions, rancours, follies, boastings, intoxications, of humanity—in short, as negligible as all the inconsequences and aberrations in the history of humanity. Royer-Collard—that King of Pedants—solemnly declared: "I know nothing more despicable than a fact." But for Cavour a fact meant everything. His mind, his eye, his mental and visual organs, were so ordered that in the complex tissue of events he saw only effective realities. Tocqueville, on the other hand, based his arguments upon political and social phenomena solely for the pure pleasure of arguing ; facts interested him only in so far as ideas might be derived from them, as they might be interpolated into a theoretical demonstration or a preconceived synthesis. Cavour regarded observation and analysis as preliminary states only ; his dialectics never delayed him for an instant if he saw no hope of thereby uncovering the motive of an action, the element of a design, or a principle of conduct. In every political crisis he saw not an ideology to construct, but a governmental problem to solve. Tocqueville was a dreamer ; Cavour a man of action.

After five months' absence, Cavour returned to Piedmont and again resumed his agricultural activities. But his journey had had a profound effect on his life. Through being brought into touch with new forms of modern society he became irrevocably fixed in his determination one day to enter political life. But the time was not yet. Indeed, as the Austrian yoke pressed ever more heavily upon Italy, that time seemed to sink beyond a far and misty horizon. In Piedmont as in Lombard Venetia, in the duchies of Parma, Modena, and Tuscany, in the Papal States, and in the Neapolitan kingdom, the same tyranny held sway ; the same despotic administration ; the same moral and intellectual oppression. Cavour, then, returned to the land. And in order that he might the better devote himself to it, he obtained permission from his father to manage, in addition to those he had previously managed at Grinzane and Santéna, his vast estate at Léri in the province of Verceil between the Po and the Sésia. The land was extremely fertile but, uniformly divided into rice-fields and pastures, was flat, ugly, and monotonous. Cavour installed himself with three servants in a plain farmhouse on the estate, and adapted himself with difficulty to a life that he found trying in spite of frequent visits to Turin.

Sometimes in the tedium of winter, when the mists hung heavy on the river, gloomy bitterness enveloped him. " I'm good for nothing," he said. " Politically speaking, my life is over. All avenues of approach are closed to me. I should be a fool were I to be duped again by dreams of power and glory such as those that fed my youth ! What folly it all was ! Henceforth I must make a virtue of necessity, and resign myself for the rest of my days to the peaceful life of a Piedmontese farmer, of an honest burgher of Turin ! " One evening a sudden access of melancholy plunged him into great distress—not the distress of the passive soul that sinks under the bludgeonings of Fate, but the fierce and rebellious distress of the proud nature suddenly detesting an ignoble life. He wept " tears of anger " ; he contemplated suicide. " My death," he wrote in his diary, " would have an excellent effect on many people. My nephews would be warned against spiritual pride, love of too much independence and the pernicious temptations of vanity." It was near Léri in a monastery of Verceil that in the thirteenth century the *Imitation of Christ* was written. The unknown and enlightened monk who wrote out this mystic's breviary, this perfect textbook of asceticism and resignation, put his readers as well as himself on guard against arrogance of spirit, the lure of freedom, and the snares of vanity. More, he denounced the great dangers of carnal temptation and, as it is written in Ecclesiastes, the terrible danger " of giving one's substance to women " (*Ne dederis mulieribus substantiam tuam !*).

Had Cavour taken this last advice to heart, he would certainly never have felt, even in passing, that passionate distaste of life, that violent temptation to find refuge in death. But from his earliest youth, his infancy, he had lain under the spell of Woman. At the age of six, on 11 May 1816, he wrote to one of his little friends, a baby girl :

" MY DEAR FANCHONETTE,

I am very sorry I have not written to you ; I confess my idleness. But why have you deserted me ? What a wrong you have done me ! I love you always and call you my Fanchonette. But now I have made friends with a young, charming, and affecting lady ; her name is Juliette de Barolo ; she has twice come to take me for a drive in her beautiful gilded carriage.

" Good-bye ! Au revoir ! Good night ! Good evening !
Your little friend,
CAMILLE."

There is nothing extraordinary about this sentimental precocity ; it is commonly found in those who later reveal themselves great lovers. Thus Dante, when at the age of nine he first encountered Beatrice : " Whenever I saw her my heart beat so violently that the blood shuddered in the least of my veins. Since that day love has been my master. . . ." In or about their tenth year Rousseau, Alfieri, Novalis and

Heinrich Heine experienced their first emotions in the
presence of womanly beauty. Byron was only eight when
he conceived for a little girl, Mary Duff, a passion so violent
" that I do not believe "—as he later confessed—" I have
ever experienced a similar." Cavour's feelings in their
premature awakening did not play him false. " The young
and affecting lady " who made him forget Fanchonette, the
Marchioness Barolo, *née* Colbert, was worthy of his naïve
devotion. As elegant and amiable as she was lively and
distinguished, she possessed a rare charm that made her
salon the first in Turin for taste, birth, and entertainment.
There is no doubt that she divined what it was that troubled
the heart of her young admirer, for from that time she
interested herself in the child, displaying towards him a
maternal tenderness—also, perhaps, the indefinable sentiments of the Comtesse Almaviva for Chérubin. Later, she
became his best friend, his chosen confidante ; it was she
who in 1832 received the prophetic letter in which he un-
veiled his secret conviction, naïvely avowing that he would
think it quite natural " to wake up one fine morning Prime
Minister of the Kingdom of Italy." In the intimate memories
of this beautiful creature, so praised, so loved, what passionate
declaration could equal such an avowal ?

From the day when he left the Military Academy at
Turin his gallantries were beyond all reckoning ; he was
always worshipping at a woman's shrine ; his youthful
passions grew, wore out, and again revived. To the gallantries succeeded the great love-affair. It overwhelmed him
at Genoa in the person of the Marchioness Giustiniani. No
sooner did they meet than they knew themselves to be

destined for one another. Of old Genoese blood, related by marriage to a ducal patrician family, twenty-five years of age, the Marchioness Anna Giustiniani exercised a great fascination upon all with whom she came into contact, less by the beauty of her features, which were not regular, than by the brilliance of her manners and her charm, her dream-drowned eyes, the sparkling animation of her face, her high courage, her fine and liberal wealth of feeling. Politically, she professed an ardent liberalism, and longed for and demanded with an impatient heart the enfranchisement of the Italian people. It was upon this noble theme that she first felt herself in harmony with Cavour; this was, as Francesca de Rimini says, " the first beginning of their love " (*la prima radice del nostro amore*). Before the image of a crucified country " the first sighs " rose to their lips and they became aware of " vague desires " :

> *Al tempo de' dolci sospiri,*
> *A che, e come concedette amore,*
> *Che conosceste i dubbiosi desiri.*

But their joy was short-lived. Hardly had they tasted of it when fate separated them with brusque hand. Cavour was sent to do penance at the fort at Bard ; then he resigned his commission ; and, finally, he embarked on his career as " gentleman farmer " at Grinzane and Santéna. Four years passed without their seeing each other. Gradually they ceased writing, and soon knew nothing more of each other. Then Cavour accidentally heard that she was in Milan, and very ill. Though he no longer felt for her " any sentiment of love," the news deeply affected him. Of their recent

liaison all that remained to him was " the desire to dedicate
a sincere and disinterested friendship to this noble woman."
Was all then at an end between them? No; their real
romance was yet to come.

On 5 July 1834 Cavour was at Grinzane, where for no
special reason he had for some time been in a mood of sadness
and despondency. One morning a letter was brought to
him addressed in a hand that made his heart leap in his
breast. The Marchioness Giustiniani informed him that she
was at Turin, and would like to see him. Let Cavour tell
in his own words what followed. He entered even the
most insignificant details in his diary; but a fine discretion
withheld him from mentioning the Marchioness by name.
He gave her the pseudonym of " l'Incognita." When he
first saw the letter his heart smote him so strongly that for
a moment he thought he would faint. " I have no words
to describe the feelings that agitated me at that moment.
Uncertainty as to the motives that had inspired l'Incognita to
this step troubled me cruelly. Had she thought of nothing
but of explaining her past conduct to me and of re-establishing
friendly contact with me? Or had she come anew under
the sway of this passion against which she had for so long
and vainly struggled? I thought to detect in her short note
a tenderness barely concealed. Yet this might be only an
illusion created by my own feelings or vanity, for there was
not a single word that spoke of any change in my favour.
I could not resist it. Leaving fifty matters that demanded
my attention, braving a sun so hot as hardly to be borne, I
was on the road within an hour. Having changed horses at
Brà without stopping, I arrived in Turin shortly after eight

o'clock. I hastened home, changed my dress, and lost no time in flying to the hotel where l'Incognita was staying. I was told she had just gone to the Opera. I hastened there; I dashed into the pit; in the sixth box in the left front row I saw a lady in deep mourning, bearing upon the sweetest of faces marks of long and cruel suffering: it was she! She recognised me at once and followed me with her eyes as I left the pit to join her. Good God! the charm of that look! The tenderness and love! Whatever the future allows me to do for her, ah! I shall never be able to requite her for all the happiness that look gave me! Her box was full of people who wearied my poor love with the most insipid of talk. Our eyes vainly sought to express the feeling surging in our hearts. We were consumed with impatience; but at last we were left alone for a moment. Alas! the myriad things we had to say to one another stifled the words in our throats. After a long silence she asked: 'What did you think of me?' 'Can you ask what I thought of you?' I replied. 'You have suffered.' 'Oh, yes, I have indeed suffered!' These are the only words I can remember. That evening I left her full of hope, of love, of regret, of remorse. I believed in the constancy of love; I was proud and intoxicated by a love so pure, so disinterested; but when I dwelt on the terrible suffering she had endured for my sake, and when I saw its traces on her beautiful face, I flew into a fury with myself, accusing myself of insensibility, of cruelty, of baseness. . . ."

On leaving the Opera the lovers arranged to meet the next evening. When he returned home, Cavour learnt quite by chance that his father, ignorant of his arrival in

4

Turin, purposed leaving his castle at Santéna at dawn the
next day in order to visit Grinzane. " Wishing to spare
him a useless journey, I at once set off on foot as there was
no carriage to be had. It was midnight; the moon shone
soft and brilliant; the banks of the Po, the hill of Turin,
bathed in her pale and melancholy light, were magical with
a beauty in harmony with my thoughts. What a glorious
walk! When shall I capture again emotions so pure and
high! . . . At Montcalieri I was able to hire a carriage; I
arrived at Santéna at three o'clock in the morning." Returning to Turin by the evening of the same day, he at
once went to l'Incognita's hotel. " I went up, I entered,
and found her alone, seated near her table. Her air of deep
despondency, her dark clothing, made a very mournful
impression upon me. She was sadness personified. What
was the cause of this sadness? . . . At first she received me
with constraint, without a word of reproach. I stammered
a few words of excuse. At last, emboldened by the sweetness
of her look, I took her hand and, carrying it to my lips,
said : ' Do you forgive me? ' She could not long resist ;
she bent her head, resting her forehead on her hand; her
sorrowful mouth sought mine with a kiss of love and peace."
He left her in a rapture of happiness, in a lyrical abandonment
of gratitude. " Am I honoured by such a love? Ah! I
vow I never, never will leave this divine woman again. I
will consecrate my life to her. Henceforth I will strive for
her alone. May the curse of Heaven fall upon me if I ever
do this perfect and adorable soul the least hurt! "

Four days later life, cruel life, separated them again.
Poor Incognita! She had expanded on this adventure what

little strength remained to her, and was obliged to go for a long rest to Vinadio in the Alps. From there, fevered and trembling, she wrote to her lover : " These three days spent with you have blotted out the memory of cruel years. I tell you, Camille, that I am but your own reflection ; without you I am nothing, I cease to exist. They need not hope to separate me from you ! Parents, friends, I would renounce them all rather than cease from seeing you. Perhaps I shall have many burdens to bear ; but I foresee them without being afraid ; I know that nothing can cast me down, as long as I am sure of your love, and I am sure of it ! . . . If I have deceived myself, I will sink to the dust before unde-ceiving myself ! But no, Camille knows how to love ; Camille will never want to hurt me ; he is too great, too generous. Soon I shall have covered the space that separates us ; soon I shall be in your arms ! " Alone with the dream that consumed her, her passion increased hourly. On 22 July she wrote to Cavour : " I was very troubled yesterday, and I reproach myself for it. You saw how weak I was, and how susceptible to fear. My vain terrors are gone now, and I no longer fear the future. I shall take care of my life, shall always reverence it, since you attach value to it. But do not think me quite worthy of the devotion you have for me. Our positions are so different ! Fate has marked you as my last stay, you, strong, talented ; *has called you perhaps to the most brilliant of careers.* My life is almost ended ; yours has just begun. I accept your heaven-sent help. Yet it is my duty to tell you what may seem a sacrifice on my part, but on the contrary is an act of pure egoism, while the same action in you would have its source in a devotion I do not merit. I have said enough: you will understand. I am tired. I am going back to bed. Goodbye! I adore you!"

Already Death had set his seal upon her. She had contracted a deadly disease, deadly and devouring; she wore next her delicate breast the rough sackcloth that could not be removed; she was one of that tragic army of great lovers who live only for their love and who die for it—the deathless army of which the heroines, through the ages, are named Medea, Ariadne, Dido, Yseult, Héloïse, the Princesse de Clèves, the Portuguese Nun, Julie de Lespinasse, Elvira.

L'Incognita, like all sensitive souls whose mental faculties have been hypersensitised by an absorbing interest, had moments of prophetic vision. Thus, though on 22 July 1834 Cavour was only a young man of twenty-four, a commissionless lieutenant, a younger son, unknown, earning his living indifferently well by managing the paternal estates, l'Incognita nevertheless divined that a great future awaited him, and predicted for him " the most brilliant of careers." From this prediction she proceeded to another that spelt for her a sentence of death: " Our positions are so different! . . . My life is almost ended; yours has just begun! . . ." She foresaw the insurmountable obstacles, the fatal incompatibilities soon to disunite them. Another like her, Sophie de Monnier, seized with the same presentiment, wrote to Mirabeau: " You are only twenty-six. Soon love will no longer be the one thing in your life. Ambition calls you, and is seducing you."

They were right—these two women. After all, closely considered, Cavour had several traits in common with

Mirabeau. The same physique, the same virile instincts, the same sensual imagination and voluptuous tastes. The lover of the Marchioness Giustiniani could have written this aphorism inserted in the *Lettres de Vincennes* : " Why do all loves, even the most tender, have an end ? Because one thinks to taste pleasures which are never to be found in them. And this because in mortal man the imagination is more active than the heart is sensitive."

The happiness of l'Incognita was once again more nearly menaced than she knew. After several weeks of ideal tenderness and high romance, Cavour suddenly disappeared. He had been ensnared by a Piedmontese Circe, an astute and depraved coquette (*una consumata e sensuale civettona*), who in a mood of boastfulness and perverse spitefulness had thrown herself in the way of the voluptuous Camille for the cruel pleasure of torturing the Marchioness Giustiniani. She gave herself altogether and at once, inflaming him by skilful ardours, and, glorying in her triumph, appeared publicly as his avowed mistress. Henceforth the life of l'Incognita became a prolonged sacrifice. Five years she spent in dying. Inconsolable, shrinking even from her family, she vanished into the silence and solitude that surrounds a shade. When Death at last drew nigh, she made a supreme effort, sending her faithless lover, this dignified farewell : " The woman who loved you is dead ; she had no beauty left, for she had suffered greatly. She knew better than you wherein she had failed. I repeat : she is dead. And in the realm of Death she has met old rivals. If she yielded the palm to them for beauty in a world where the senses are so easily seduced, here she surpasses them all. . . . And now good-bye, Camille !

As I write these lines I am unshaken in my resolve never to see you again. You will read them, I hope. And when an insurmountable barrier shall have arisen between us, when I have been initiated into the secrets of the grave, then, perhaps (I shudder to think of it!) I shall have forgotten you."

Although Cavour's amours were numerous, they have scarcely more than an episodic importance for his biographer. Yet they cannot altogether be ignored, since they bear witness not only to his physical virility but also to the numerous traits of mind and personality, the many little idiosyncrasies, to which he was presently to owe his success in politics. For example: his strong emotionalism, his calculated readiness to accept risks, his exact conception of the object he was pursuing, his perseverance in its pursuit, his skill in manipulating a situation for his own ends, his rapid power of recovery after a rebuff, his keen appreciation and understanding of human psychology, his promptness and ability to seize an opportunity, and finally his intuitive sense of when to make, and his courage in making, the decisive move. But in order to understand how he came to hold the opinions he did, and the school in which he was prepared for his political career, one must observe him as an agriculturist at Léri. Let us watch him then about the year 1843 when his agricultural experiments were beginning to produce remarkable results—see him as he appeared to his occasional visitors or his hunting companions. In its rustic simplicity the life he led was one of great ease and comfort: " A life of the farm and not of the castle," wrote one of his friends, a keen sportsman. " Late to bed and early to rise, short days, dinners cooked by the old housekeeper, who herself brought the great dishes of smoking game and risotto to the heavy oak table around which, after dessert, we gathered to play lansquenet. In those days we never complained of the flatness and dullness of the country-side, or of the miasma that rose up from the rice-fields. For what crops were grown in those rice-fields ! What herds were raised in the plains ! What a whirring of machinery was to be heard in the sheds ! What a scene of activity in the farmyard ! What well-filled granaries ! What prosperity everywhere ! " These remarkable results were the reward of ten years of labour— of a ten years' battle against man and nature ; against heat and rain ; against miasma ; against all the forces with which, since the days of Triptolemus, the earth has resisted all new methods to increase her productivity ; and against the ignorance and prejudice of the peasants. Cavour was proud of his achievement. " If you could only understand," he wrote to a friend, " what peace, what keen satisfaction there is in a well-cultivated field or in a pasture covered with close herbage ! " Another time he wrote : " Each day I appreciate more the sedative influence of rural life. In every way it satisfies my practical instincts. Agriculture has for me the fascination of a science." From these and other similar confidences it would be easy to infer that Cavour had found his vocation and abandoned his political ambitions. But in truth it was quite the contrary. In a delightful psychological novel entitled *Dominique*, Fromentin depicts a man of fine tastes and generous aspirations who at the age of thirty has failed to fulfil the ambitions of his youth. He retires to his country estates to seek in a rural life that which it withholds from none—a sense of balance, a calm, a quiet acceptance of the irrefragable decrees of Fate. But what a difference exists between the resignation that led Dominique to Trembles and that which sent Cavour to Léri! Dominique is not only averse to an active life; he has taken stock of himself and, having deemed himself worthless, he has irrevocably renounced the world. In mourning for his dreams, he seeks as a last exercise of his pride to identify himself completely with the anonymous crowd of " negative quantities." His renouncement becomes an irrevocable and complete abdication. With Cavour, on the other hand, renouncement was only of a temporary character—" for a time." Force of circumstances, and not he himself, had imposed it upon him. Although compelled to postpone their realisation, he never abandoned his dreams. Hence his frequent outbursts of impatience; his temporary fits of depression. Of these Dominique showed no trace; nor the least sign of revolt. Only an absolute passivity. Hence while the Lord of Trembles occupied himself with melancholy evocations of the past, Cavour's gaze was firmly fixed upon the future.

But what picture of the future had he in his mind? What sort of career did he foresee for himself? Two journeys to Paris and London about this time seem to have hastened the development and the clarifying of his ideas. What he had observed in France and England showed him that modern society was " turning fatally towards democracy," and that " to try to arrest the course of events would be to unleash the tempest without any chance of bringing the ship back to harbour." The chimera of democracy did not impose upon him; he feared neither collective tyranny nor individual despotism; he had no faith in "the political genius of mobs"; he held in particular distrust their constant desire for innovation; and he condemned in advance all progress not brought about lawfully and in order, under the control of a legitimate power whose roots were struck deep in the history of the country." In these words he defined the liberal State.

Another consideration engrossed his attention with even greater force. His travels in France and England, where he especially sought opportunities for conversing with financiers, industrialists, shipowners, and merchants, revealed to him with the vividness of a dream the important part that economic phenomena played at that time in the life of nations. On his return, feeling the need of clarifying his ideas, he took his pen and wrote a treatise on *British Corn Laws*, denouncing with astonishing justness the errors and dangers of Protection. Sir Robert Peel himself used no more persuasive arguments when opening the grave debate in the House of Commons two years later. But Cavour did not stop there; he had too practical a mind to be contented with theories and speculations. He set himself to work without delay, and within a few months he was to be found organising committees and conferences on agriculture; a company for the export of flour; a manure factory; a bank of exchange; a chemical factory. But the problem that interested him above all others was that of the railways.

It was only in November 1845 that a financial syndicate received powers to construct between Genoa and Turin the first railway to run on Piedmontese soil. Cavour naturally took a keen interest in it and was one of the chief share-

holders.   But his vivid imagination at once perceived an
infinity of remote and transcendent possibilities arising from
the undertaking as already planned.   Before his eyes there
arose a vision of a vast network of railways stretching little
by little far beyond the narrow frontiers of his Cisalpine
fatherland to the extreme limits of the Peninsula.   Hence
the necessity that the construction and route of each individual
line should be in accord with a general plan that should keep
a possible future unification in view.   This, however, was
not enough.   The Italy of the future must be prepared to
take an active part in European transport ; a way must be
cut through the Alps at several places, and, most urgent
need of all, a tunnel must be bored through Mont Cenis.
Obviously it was the conception of a united Italy that inspired
this vast technical programme ; it was stated quite openly
in the end.   Important as the material benefits might be
from a network of railways spread over all Italy, Cavour
thought them much inferior to the moral advantages which
would inevitably spring from it.

From what cause had sprung those evils that through the
centuries had tormented the Italian people and placed them
under the heel of a foreign oppressor?   Is it not to be
found in the internecine struggles, the rivalry between the
petty States, the fratricidal warfare that render Italian history
so bloodstained and pitiful ?   But when a network of railways covered the Peninsula from Turin to Venice, from
Milan to Naples, the diverse races who had formerly hated
or ignored one another would be obliged to unite, to mingle,
to understand one another, and to work together.   Rapidly
forgetting their provincial rivalries, they would attain to a

consciousness of national unity and come to possess a national soul. On the day when that came to pass the era of national freedom would at last begin. Nothing would then be able to obstruct Italy's advancement. History reveals that a preliminary and necessary condition for the intellectual, economic, and moral regeneration of a people is the full expansion of its nationality.

In May 1846 Cavour made himself the self-appointed advocate of this great scheme which terrified the timorous officials of Turin. Charles Albert at one moment thought of exiling his former page, whom he declared to be " the most dangerous man in the kingdom." Nor was the accusation unjust : Cavour had indeed become dangerous. The intensely active life he had led for some years past, accompanied as it was by an intense and systematic concentration upon numerous and divergent interests, had (so to speak) borne a rich harvest. The idea of an independent Italy had little by little grown up in him. It is true that he was not its originator, that it was not his exclusive possession. Many of his compatriots, among them d'Azeglio, Gioberti, Balbo, Mazzini, had held it for a long time past ; but none of them had thought of it in so precise a form, so objectively, with so clear a perception of eventualities and practical necessities. This idea had become the dominating force in his life, engaging all his intelligence and will-power in its service, and summoning him to action. It ruled his entire spirit ; it animated his sleeping and waking thoughts ; it rose up in his soul as an indestructible and certain hope, as a towering and invincible fortress. *Arx animæ.*

CHAPTER II

THE FIRST ADVENTURE

CHAPTER II

THE FIRST ADVENTURE

"WILL the hour never strike?" wrote Mirabeau in a frenzy of impatience. For more than fifteen years the agriculturist of Léri had known this fever of soul.

On 26 June 1848 the road to a political career was at last opened to him. At an election he simultaneously offered himself as a candidate in four constituencies, of which Turin was one. Elected by all four, he chose to sit for his natal city. Soon afterwards the Chamber was dissolved, and he lost his seat, only to reconquer it, after a hard fight, on 9 December 1849. From that day until his death Cavour represented Turin in the Carignan Palace.

It was a tragic hour. The army of Piedmont had been routed on the field of Novara. Crushed by his misfortunes, seeking death in vain upon the battlefield, Charles Albert on the evening of Novara laid down his crown and left his kingdom, to die some months later in asceticism and saintliness near Oporto. Victorious all along the line, masters of Tanaro and the Sésin, with no more formidable foe than a panic-stricken army before them, the Austrians dictated a Draconian peace. At this hour democratic passions became inflamed at Turin, where Brofferio, the leader of the " reds," proclaimed the world-revolution. At Genoa it was the same. Everywhere revolution, separatism, anarchy. Piedmont in those dark days seemed to have fallen into utter ruin.

This fact must be borne in mind when making a study of Cavour the statesman : his point of departure for political life, the land that occasion offered on which to lay the foundations of his great national edifice, was a little vanquished kingdom, ruined, invaded, true to itself, yet ridiculous in the eyes of the world because of the foolhardy temerity of its latest adventure.

On the morrow of the disaster the political programme of Cavour could be summed up in a sentence : To maintain the d'Azeglio Ministry which had undertaken the mournful task of making peace with Austria and which was valiantly endeavouring to re-establish law and order without forfeiting a single constitutional guarantee. This last point Cavour regarded as of great importance: " As long as liberty lives on in a single corner of the Peninsula," he declared, " I shall never lose hope of the future. As long as Piedmont guards her Constitution and traditions from the assaults of despotism and anarchy, we shall be able to save the nation." Never throughout his life did Cavour conceive of the restoration of his country as capable of achievement save by the free play of constitutional forces. Nor was this solely because his personal predilections had attached him to liberal ideas. First and foremost it was because he saw in representative government the best way in which to attract to Piedmont all the scattered forces of Italian nationalism; because if the other sovereigns of the Peninsula were no longer under the influence of a reactionary Austria, it mattered little which of them might seek to assume the rôle that Victor Emmanuel was about to fill; which might seek to claim for his house the honour of snatching Italy from humiliation and servitude.

This high political conception did not prevent the new deputy from devoting his attention to the more pressing problems involved in the financial ruin of the kingdom. On this subject he soon revealed himself a master; and when he intervened in a financial debate in the Chamber he dominated that assembly. Hence when Count Santa Rosa, the Minister for Commerce, died suddenly on 11 October 1850, Cavour was designated by all as his successor. On his name being proposed to the King by d'Azeglio, Victor Emmanuel stared at the proposer with his large and shrewd eyes: " Do you wish me to nominate Cavour ? " he asked. " For my part, I should like to. But rest assured he will take all your portfolios ! " And in fact Cavour soon gathered into his own hands the portfolios of Commerce, Agriculture, the Navy, and Finance.

Far from overwhelming him, this multiplicity of affairs only served to make him great. His unprejudiced knowledge of economics, the breadth of his reforming ideas, his wealth of knowledge and vigorous, spirited eloquence, his keenness and animation, indeed his whole magnetic personality, made him, in fact, the Prime Minister of Piedmont. Towards the close of 1852, after a parliamentary crisis had resulted in the formation of a great Liberal-Conservative party, Cavour replaced d'Azeglio as President of the Council. His nomination bears date 4 November 1852. That same day the French Senate was summoned to deliberate on the re-establishment of the Empire. By a fatidical coincidence the two chief actors in the Italian drama came simultaneously upon the stage.

5

CHAPTER III

CAVOUR AND THE SPHINX

CAVOUR AND THE SPHINX

" IN certain cases the wise man leaves much to chance; reason prompts him to follow blindly after impulses or instincts beyond reason, and that seem to be heaven-sent. No man can say when these should be dared or when deserted; nor book, nor rules, nor experience can teach him; a certain sense and a certain daring alone can inform him." Thus Louis XIV expressed himself in his Memoirs. But, indeed, the very mention of his name is superfluous, since it is impossible to conceive of anyone else who could have formulated such a precept of governance with such absolute authority. The royal aphorism applies with great exactitude to Cavour at the time when Destiny first granted him an opportunity in which to translate his patriotic ideas into actions. That opportunity came with the outbreak of the Crimean War in the spring of 1854. The part he then played in European diplomacy revealed his most marked characteristic and the determining cause of his future actions : audacity. From early youth he had displayed a passion for gambling that had often cost him dear. Cards and the Stock Exchange had been his constant preoccupation. His passion certainly did not spring from a sordid love of gain, for no one could have been more generous, even spendthrift; rather it sprang from a desire to tempt fortune and provoke the capriciousness of Chance. Born a man of action, Cavour naturally became a gambler; for every grave action implies not only an anticipation of the future but a claim to be able to decide events, to lead and to control them. Thus Lucretius was led to declare all human effort to be "a violent tilt at Fate" (*fatis avulsa potestas*).

Moreover, as Louis XIV so exactly put it, the audacity of a great statesman has nothing in common with the rash impulse of a foolhardy spirit. Rather should it be inspired by wisdom and counselled by reason, for it consists in a perfect union of intellect and will; of imagination and common sense; of courage and reflection. Of this audacity Cromwell, and not Napoleon, is the finest personification. For the great genius of Napoleon, his love for the gigantic and his passion for war, too often led him to indulge in the terrible hazard of battle. Cromwell, on the other hand, even in his most daring decisions, showed himself always a cool and careful calculator; at the height of his pride and ambition he never lost control of his actions. In this respect Cavour stands next to Cromwell.

Even to-day, after the passage of years and with the benediction of success upon it, the idea of involving the tiny Piedmont, still crippled from Novara, in the Crimean War, is not a little surprising. Nor is it to be wondered at that contemporary observers should at first sight have regarded it as absurd. Since his advent to power Cavour had won for himself a reputation for the possession of solid qualities— capacity for work, force of character, an intelligence of a high order, a healthy positivism, and common sense. But now his action seemed devoid of reason. His cousin La Rive has ably given expression to the thoughts of the wiser among his contemporaries when they learned that Piedmont was going to war with so great and so distant an enemy as Russia. " In time of peace," wrote La Rive, " neither at the bidding of popular passion nor external force, coldly, and in the secrecy of solitary meditations, he (Cavour) determined to engage his country in a war of which he could know neither the result nor the duration, and in which the interests of his country were so indirectly involved that it seemed necessary even to find a pretext for being engaged in it ; then, having taken this decision, he imposed it on his unwilling colleagues, on a frightened Parliament, and on a hostile public opinion. It was, indeed, one of those audacious acts hateful only to those who think that their ships carry Cæsar and his fortune." In reality, Cavour had for long meditated taking this audacious decision. In 1851, as Minister for Commerce, Cavour had sought to gain the sympathy of France under the cloak of commercial relations. In seeking the assent of the Parliament to a reduction of the tariffs as a concession to French protectionism, he propounded to his astonished hearers a sibylline argument. " All around us the horizon is dark. An event may arise that will cause us to desire the support of France. This is the consideration that has induced me in the commercial treaty that lies before you, not to sacrifice economic considerations, but to relegate them to the second place ; these are the political ideas that more than any others have inspired me." He concluded his speech with an amazing prophecy : " It is not impossible that the future will bring forth a European convulsion of so great dimensions that East and West will be split into two camps. How shall we stand in that day unless we are on terms of good friendship with France?" Three years later the "convulsion" had become a reality; Europe was broken in two; and the quarrel over the Holy Places, more truly, over the recurring question of the ownership of Constantinople, once again ranged the armed forces of a large part of Western Europe against the East.

Ever since the Anglo-French ultimatum to Russia in March 1854, Cavour was as one hypnotised by the events taking place on the shores of the Black Sea—events which bore in their train humiliating disasters and severe hardships for the allied armies. Even before the expeditionary force, which had escaped disaster in the Dobroudja, had been sent to besiege Sevastopol, Cavour had perceived the great opportunity Fortune was daily offering to Piedmont. The clever and spirited Marchioness Alfieri, who was his favourite niece and in whose company he passed his evenings, asked him point-blank: "Why do you not send ten thousand men to the Crimea?" She had rightly divined his thought, for he started, his eyes lit up, and with a sigh he replied: "Ah! if everyone had your courage the thing would have been done." During the following autumn, when the terrible slaughter at Balaclava and Inkerman had shown the Allies that they were still far from a decisive victory and that such a victory would cost them dear, the sprightly Marchioness once more interrogated her uncle. This time he maintained an obstinate silence. "Well!" she cried. "When are we leaving for the Crimea?" "Who knows?" came the reply. "For England and France are pressing me to conclude a treaty which will give our army the chance to wipe out the stain of Novara. But what can be done?

My Cabinet will not hear of it. Even Rattazzi and my good friend La Marmora have threatened to resign. . . . The King fortunately is on my side, and together we shall manage it."

Actually, he had himself won over the King. A soldier in every inch of his body, impatient to wipe the stain of Novara and of 1849 from the shield of Savoy, Victor Emmanuel had at once supported Cavour's idea and had devoted all his energy to winning acceptance for it. In an audience he granted to the French minister, the Duc de Gramont, the King had gone so far as to say to him : " I will send my soldiers to Sevastopol. My ministers, indeed, do not wish me to do so ; but Cavour is on my side, and if necessary I will change my ministers. Then my troops shall go and, at that moment when they stand shoulder to shoulder with yours, I will set Austria at defiance." Cavour, on the other hand, had taken great pains to win over public opinion and the Parliament to his cause. Among all sections of the populace the sending of an army corps to the Crimea was looked upon as a hare-brained idea. " Why should we involve ourselves in this war ? By so doing we shall gain neither glory nor profit. We shall be in the pay and at the mercy of our Allies. Were this demanded of us, it would be more than absurd : it would be a crime against the fatherland. After Novara, Piedmont should not shed a drop of blood, except in defence." But to this Cavour replied : " It is regard for national interests, and nothing else, that inspires me. We must show Europe that we can fight and that we have not lost our valour. Believe me, the laurels which our troops will win in the Crimea will be worth more for the future of Italy than all the oratory in the world."

But his negotiations in Paris and London were not un-attended by difficulties. He did not wish to involve Pied-mont in war before obtaining from his allies a proof, implicit if not expressed, of their sympathy with Italian aspirations. That he was finally successful in this was due to his diplomatic gifts no less than to his perseverance and ingenuity. On 10 January 1855 he signed the protocols by which Piedmont was made an ally of Great Britain and France, and which fixed the strength of the Piedmontese expeditionary force at 18,000 men. In affixing his signature, Cavour was staking his political career. He knew it, for on the following day he wrote to Count Oldofredi: "I have taken a terrible responsibility upon myself. It does not matter. Let what-ever may come, come! My conscience tells me I have fulfilled a sacred duty." That he knew what risk he ran is shown by the fact that he made preparations in advance for the loss of his personal property. If his policy miscarried or if, through his mistake, the blood of his fellow-countrymen was spilt in vain, he would vanish from public life; he would become an exile. To his great friend in Paris, Madame de Circourt, he confided: "My ridiculous and romantic policy will presently be judged. If I fall, you will not refuse me an asylum." But, after some misfortunes, all his hopes, all his calculations, were realised. Led by a military genius in the person of La Marmora, the tiny Pied-montese army played a brilliant part in the Crimea. On 16 August 1855 it covered itself with glory at the Tchernaia, and French and British alike were prodigal in their praises

VICTOR EMMANUEL II.

of its valour. Novara was effaced and forgotten. Then on
8 September there came the capture of the Malakoff and the
fall of Sevastopol.

Before negotiations for peace were formally opened and
while a possible resumption of hostilities still hung in the
balance, Victor Emmanuel, on the invitation of Napoleon III,
visited Paris to view the great Exhibition which had recently
been visited by Queen Victoria and the Prince Consort.
Cavour accompanied his Royal master, and on 23 November
the King and his suite were lodged in the Tuileries. For six
days receptions, galas, and fêtes in the glittering and ostenta-
tious style of the Second Empire succeeded one another.
Wherever he went Victor Emmanuel attracted the gaze of
the crowd. With his little grey eyes looking out from his
big face, his enormous moustaches sweeping upwards to
form a great crescent, his squat shoulders and corpulence,
and his fierce mien, he was deemed ugly. Nevertheless his
frank and open manner no less than the good-nature
which lay hidden beneath his rough exterior earned for him
universal respect. Nor was the heroism he had displayed
at Novara forgotten any more than the courage with
which he had ascended the throne amidst the dismay
caused by that disaster. Then, too, he belonged to the
most ancient reigning house in Europe, and to his pride
of race united a noble chivalry and a high conception of
his kingly duty.

The old Comtesse Damrémont, widow of the General
who was killed on the breach at Constantine, wrote to
Thouvenel, then ambassador at Constantinople : " You know,
of course, my dear Ambassador, the kind of success King

Victor Emmanuel has had here. But in case you have not been told it *all*, I should like to tell you these little tales to divert you in your exile. The King appears to have lived more in camps than in courts. When wishing to compliment the Empress, he said that *in her presence he suffered the tortures of Tantalus* : to Princess Mathilde that *she set him aflame* ; that he had expected to be received by her behind *closed doors*, and that the *open curtains embarrassed him prodigiously*. One day, in the Empress's circle, the King went straight up to Mme de Malaret, a Lady-in-waiting, and said: '*Good-day, Madame. I like Frenchwomen, and have observed since my sojourn in Paris that they dress other than the ladies of Turin. Here the approaches to Paradise are open.*' You will understand how the poor woman longed that the floor would open and swallow her, and how the whole *salon* was convulsed with merriment. On the closing day of the Exhibition, the King approached M. de Morny : 'I observe,' said he, '*that the Emperor is very popular, and especially in comparison with his clergy. It's just the opposite with me ; but* (making a pirouette); *je m'en f——.*' M. de Morny replied : '*With me too.*' Then, pirouetting in his turn, he said to those about him : '*At least here we have someone who knows French.*' I know enough of these tales to fill twenty pages of a letter. But I will finish with this one. The other evening at the Opera, Victor Emmanuel, who was seated beside the Emperor, had been staring for some time at a little dancer. Leaning towards the Emperor, he asked : '*Sire, what is the price of that little girl?*' '*I don't know,*' replied the Emperor ; '*ask Bacciochi.*' Turning, the King said : 'What is the price of that child ?' Bacciochi replied : '*Sire, to your Majesty, five thousand francs.*' '*The devil ! It's a great deal,*' returned the King. Then the Emperor, addressing Bacciochi : ' Charge it up to me.' "

While Victor Emmanuel thus gave rein to his liveliness and his passions, Cavour took advantage of what leisure was left him from his official duties to gain information in all possible ways. "I am on the move unceasingly," he wrote to his ministerial colleague Rattazzi : "Never before have I led so busy a life." He sought to win over to the Italian cause Thiers, Lord Cowley, Walewski, the bankers Péreire and Lafitte, and, above all, Prince Napoleon. But no one was interested in the misfortunes of Italy. Everyone was concentrated upon one problem : whether the war would be resumed in the Crimea, as Palmerston desired, or whether Napoleon III would be able to win the day for his pacific ideas.

On 29 November Victor Emmanuel arrived in London, where he met with a reception no less hearty and splendid than he had received in Paris. Very wisely the King kept a watch over his tongue when talking with the ladies of the Court and took pains to avoid shocking them. Queen Victoria wrote to her uncle Leopold, King of the Belgians : " He is *eine ganz besondere, abenteurliche Erscheinung* " (" an extraordinary and adventurous personality "), startling in the extreme in appearance and manner when you *first* see him, but, just as Aumale says, *il faut l'aimer quand on le connaît bien* (" one has only to know him to like him "). He is so frank, open, just, straightforward, liberal, and tolerant, with much sound good sense. He never breaks his word, and you may rely on him, but wild and extravagant, courting adventures and dangers, and with a very strange, short, rough manner, an exaggeration of that short manner of speaking which his poor brother had. He is shy in society, which makes him still more brusque, and he does not know (never having been out of his own country or even out in Society), what to say to the numbers of people who are presented to him here, and which is, I know from experience, a most odious thing. . . . He is more like a Knight or King of the Middle Ages than anything one knows nowadays." Greville, indeed, seized upon this last trait as being the most characteristic of Victor Emmanuel when he compared him to a duke of the Lombards or a chief of the Herulæ, to a Hildebrand or an Odoacer.

Meanwhile, with the same activity he had displayed in Paris, Cavour began in political circles in England his work of gaining information. He questioned Palmerston, Malmesbury, Clarendon, and all the other political chiefs. But once again his reward was small. A few polite expressions, nothing more. On 6 December, on their homeward journey, Victor Emmanuel and his suite again stayed in Paris. On the following day there was a hunt at Compiègne, and in the evening Napoleon III, in speaking with Cavour, said to him brusquely: " Write privately to Walewski your views as to what I might do for Piedmont and Italy." A few generalisations followed from which the eventuality of a war with Austria was definitely excluded. That was all.

II

What thoughts passed through the Emperor's mind that evening at Compiègne? What practical designs lay behind the nebulous phrases he employed? What visions floated now clearly, now dimly, before his fancy? Two months and a half later when he arrived to take part in the Congress of Paris, Cavour was still in complete ignorance of the Emperor's thoughts and intentions.

On 15 February 1856, the day on which he left Turin for Paris, the outlook before Cavour was gloomy indeed. Not only was he in ignorance as to whether he would find an ally or an opponent in the Imperial Government; he was also troubled by a more exquisite doubt. The Great Powers, jealous of their archaic privileges, contested the right of a tiny State like Piedmont to participate in the Congress on an equal footing with themselves. They felt it beneath their dignity to deliberate in common with a paltry kingdom of 4,000,000 inhabitants. The fact that it had despatched an expeditionary force to the Crimea was of no moment. It had played no better rôle than that of a busybody. If indeed, as an act of grace, they admitted Piedmont to the Congress chamber at all, it must take a lower seat, a humble and mortifying position. Even her two Allies, even France and England, sought thus to humiliate her. But Cavour could not for an instant accept such an affront to his country. To do so would be to deal a death-blow to national aspirations. Moreover, the instructions he bore, which he had himself drafted, ordered him to leave the Congress and return to Turin, if Piedmont were not placed on a footing of perfect equality with the other Powers. It was a decisive moment in his career, a turning-point in his whole policy. Never again throughout his life did any responsibility weigh so heavily, never did a task seem so hard. His unconquerable will alone saved him from utter despondency, although his keen perception forbade him to entertain any illusions. " It is possible," he wrote, " it is even probable, that my present mission will prove to be the laſt of my public acts."

Three weeks later he had proved himself a false prophet, and his career, inſtead of being ended, was but entering upon its zenith. In the firſt place he obtained for Piedmont the right to participate in the Congress on a footing of equality with the greateſt of the Powers. For the firſt time the sacred principle of a sovereign hierarchy was violated in the diplo-matic areopagus. Metternich was effaced. Heartened by this preliminary success, Cavour commenced his campaign. On his previous visit he had contented himself with the part of an interrogator, an observer of the political terrain and horizon. Now the time had come in which to act and to manœuvre. His programme was a simple one ; but it displayed to a very high degree the character of his realism ; his objective appreciation of situations and facts ; his unfailing intuition in regard to political currents and their courses ; his prudent eſtimation of the means that lay available to his hand ; of the possibilities offered to him. Above all, he sought to create around the Piedmontese delegation an atmo-sphere of sympathy. In the early sessions of the Congress, while the great problems involved in the general terms of peace were being discussed, Cavour maintained an attitude of reserve. Yet on occasion he did not hesitate to express an opinion, though without taking sides ; and he never forgot to watch its effect upon the French and English plenipotentiaries.

But in the intervals during the formal meetings of the

Congress he was more at his ease, finding innumerable pretexts for exposing the sorrows of Italy and the crimes of Austria, and for bringing the national cause of Italy before the tribunal of public opinion. With an amazing dexterity he contrived to fill these two rôles. As he sat at the green table, he astonished and charmed his colleagues by the essential justness of his remarks, the fluency of his speech, the breadth and variety of his ideas, by his malicious smiles, silences, and allusions. He even contrived to maintain an appearance of cordial friendship with his acrimonious Austrian colleague, Count Buol. Outside the Congress he allowed himself a greater liberty of speech, pleading in innumerable ways and on all possible occasions the cause so dear to his heart. His interviews and overtures increased from day to day, and, above all, he sought to win over Lord Clarendon, Lord Cowley, Count Orloff, Prince Napoleon, and Morny. Through the intermediary of Dr. Conneau, who came of a Lombard family, he even succeeded in opening up a means of communication with the Emperor himself. In the *salons* and other resorts of the fashionable world his mission was as actively pursued, and, in pleading his cause, he brought to bear all his rare social gifts, his quickwitted and persuasive eloquence, no less than his mastery of skilful innuendo and cajolery—gifts which, as Madame de Motteville said, were the secret of Mazarin's greatness. Too worldly-wise to neglect feminine influences, he courted Princess Mathilde, the Duchesse de Bassano, Marquise de la Bédoyère, Comtesse Walewski. Nor did he forget his faithful friend Madame de Circourt. While he even found time for a romance in the midst of his political activities.

6

One evening at the Tuileries he was introduced to a
young English widow, the Marchioness of Ely, who was
Lady-in-waiting to Queen Victoria.   Tall and slender, fine of
figure, and with a lovely complexion, soft brown eyes, and
superb golden hair, the Marchioness was also clever and
charming.   So inflamed was Cavour by his passion for this
radiant vision of the eternal feminine, that to overcome her
scruples he even went the length of proposing marriage to
her.   In this love-affair his diplomatic skill came to his aid.
Between the Marchioness and her Royal mistress there
existed a close friendship, and she had been charged by the
Queen with the duty of daily reporting to her what passed
behind the scenes at the Congress.   Apart from her own
intellectual gifts, the Marchioness was specially fitted for her
task by reason of her friendship with the Montijo family and
the Empress Eugénie.   Cavour could not have found a
more suitable medium through whom confidentially to
transmit his ideas to the French and British sovereigns.

As a result of all his investigations Cavour was led to see
that the only possible way of bringing the Italian Question
before a Europe assembled in Congress was on the personal
initiative of Napoleon III.   Hence he laid before the Emperor
a memorandum " On the means by which the reconstruction
of Italy might be effected," and " On the permanent policy to
be adopted by France in the common interest of the two
countries."   Written in a concise and lucid style, this
memorandum was, in effect, the Bible of the *Risorgimento* ;
the events by which Europe was agitated for fifteen years
originated in it.   On Napoleon the memorandum made a
profound impression.   No scheme was too chimerical for his

venturesome spirit. Yet from whatever angle he studied Cavour's conclusions, they seemed even to him to be unrealisable. Sometimes it was Austria who barred the road. Sometimes it was the Pope. To embody the duchies of Parma and Modena in Piedmont would, without doubt, be a *casus belli* for Austria, while to attempt another territorial adjustment to the detriment of the Papal States by, for example, transferring Parma and Modena to Bologna and Ferrara, would render it impossible for Napoleon to seek the Papal blessing for the child whose birth he awaited. Nevertheless Cavour received an indication of what thoughts were passing in the mind of the secretive Emperor. On 16 March, at the moment when the Empress was in the pangs of childbirth and when the doctors had begun to be alarmed about her safe deliverance, the Emperor, distressed by his wife's cries, and fearful for the future of his dynasty, paced to and fro. A single remark, and a strange, fell from his lips : " Something must certainly be done for Italy ! " Three days later, when he was still intoxicated by the joy that had come to him with the birth of the Prince Imperial, he secretly summoned Cavour and Lord Clarendon to the Tuileries for an interview that lasted for two and a half hours. Of what passed at this interview little is known. Cavour indeed must have shown himself supremely tactful, clever, and importunate. For he secured a great result. The Emperor consented to bring the Italian Question before the Congress, and Clarendon promised his support.

On 8 April the bomb exploded. Peace had been signed on 27 March, and the delegates were at the end of their labours. Suddenly the shrewd and imperturbable Walewski proposed that the Congress should examine, before it dissolved, " certain subjects which were capable of giving rise to fresh troubles." Coldly he laid before it the Italian Question, from " the anomalous position of the Papal States " to the intolerable despotism which ruled in the Kingdom of Naples, and he declared that France would evacuate Rome on the day when Austria withdrew her troops from the Legations. In accordance with a preconcerted plan, Clarendon rose to support Walewski's proposal. But he did more. Speaking in a sharp and contemptuous manner, he denounced the evils of the Roman theocracy, of the King of Naples, while he lashed the effete and corrupt rule of the lesser Italian princes. Never again has a similar speech, a speech so violent and reviling, been delivered in a diplomatic assembly. In the midst of the general amazement which it occasioned Cavour arose and continued, though in a milder manner, the terrible indictment; declaring that it was not only Rome or Naples, Modena or Parma, that was at fault. The fundamental cause lay in the arrogant dominion exercised by Austria throughout the Peninsula, a dominion that had become a mortal peril to Piedmont. In vain did Count Buol on several occasions seek to stop the debate by haughtily maintaining the incompetence of the Congress to deal with these matters. He was greeted by an angry and an icy silence. Some conclusion, however, had to be arrived at. In face of the obstinate attitude maintained by Buol no practical solution could be attempted; all that could be done was to sum up the discussion in a series of vague formulas which became still more attenuated in the euphemisms of the *procès-verbal*. When this stormy session of 8 April 1856 is regarded in the light of all that came after, its capital importance is at once made manifest. For from it sprang, in logical succession, Solferino, Sadowa, and Sedan. Looked at from the standpoint of its immediate results, its importance is reduced to this : that for the first time the grievances of Italy were discussed in a European Congress and recorded in the non-committal verbiage of a protocol. That—nothing more. In Turin it was thought that the Piedmontese delegate had returned without any reward, " with not the least morsel of territory in his pocket," without the smallest recompense for the great effort put forth in the Crimea. The Opposition journals all too faithfully voiced public opinion when they wrote : " Italy should no longer build its hopes of resurrection on the European Powers. . . . The liberty of Italy will never be achieved in diplomatic congresses."

III

Cavour had, however, the right to be happy and proud, not only because he had gained for himself at the Congress of Paris a personal prestige and ascendancy which conferred on him, in the eyes of all Europe, the title of Statesman ; but because henceforward he saw his way clear before him ; because he had penetrated the nebulous meditations of Napoleon III ; because he had read the riddle of the Sphinx. It is no exaggeration to say that he had seen through him, for the Emperor revealed to him none of his thoughts. Cavour could obtain from him no promise of co-operation, no word of encouragement. Nevertheless, at the moment of parting, the sovereign allowed him to perceive that he foresaw serious complications in a not distant future : " I have a presentiment that the present peace will not last for long."

The plenipotentiary of Piedmont soon perceived that all the Emperor's usual advisers disapproved of the policy of nationalism, in which they foresaw nothing for France except the wildest of adventures. Not to mention Walewski, whose opposition had been expressed several times during the Congress, and who, during the agitated sitting of 8 April had but obeyed the imperative directions of his master; not to mention Drouyn de Lhuys, who declared himself openly in favour of the Austrian alliance; all those who had any interest in the preservation of peace were hostile to " any sort of upheaval in Europe." The faithful and waspish Persigny, ambassador in London, was one of the most tenacious in diverting the Emperor's course from combinations of a hazardous and Machiavellian nature. He expressed very true and far-seeing views on the subject : " An absolute or an impatient mind, considering the provinces of the Rhine, Italy, Poland, and Hungary, might form the thought of changing the face of Europe. For the sake of the imperial dynasty, I should deplore the birth of such a thought in the mind of the Emperor, for our dynasty no more has need of glory, but of time, and time can be replaced by nothing else. If I thought France were to be launched on a series of great undertakings, I should regret it—the greatest undertaking in the world could add nothing to the Napoleonic glory and still less could it give twenty years to the heir of the Empire." Among his intimates he expressed himself even more freely : " Let the Emperor beware of playing with the sword, for he does not know how to use it, and would cut his fingers ! The Imperial dynasty has only one chance of ruin : War."

Cavour had none the less read the mind of Napoleon III ; with the keenest penetration he had understood all that was implicitly meant in the phrase at parting : " I have a presentiment that the present peace will not last for long."

It was on 16 April 1856 that the Emperor said these words. This is a date to remember. It marks in fact a new direction in Napoleonic thought, the end of one dream and the beginning of another. In the history of the Second Empire it is the decisive turning-point. This fact is so important that it is necessary to emphasise it.

IV

When Louis Napoleon at the beginning of his presidency had begun to turn over in the innermost recesses of his mind the methods of restoring the Empire, no moral support had seemed to him to be at the same time so efficacious and so necessary as that of the French Catholics. Since the legislative elections of 13 May 1849 the Party had become reunited, and signs of their alliance had not been long in making their appearance. Immediately the Roman Expedition had changed in character. Sent forth in the preceding month to bring help to Roman liberty, its only tendency thenceforward was to overthrow the Republic of the triumvirs and to re-establish the pontifical theocracy. On 29 May General Oudinot received the order to take the offensive, and the Comte de

Falloux, " the man of the Church," became all-powerful in
the councils of the Élysée.

One can well imagine that the Prince-President had not
resigned himself without reluctance to this brusque deviation
in French policy. The famous incident of the letter to
Edgar Ney would suffice to prove how much sympathy he
still retained for the cause of the Italian Liberals, and all that
it had cost him to sacrifice it to the great plan which was
soon to crown his fortunes.

In the first place, his escapade of 1831 in the Romagna
had left an intoxicating memory in the depths of his soul.
Towards the end of 1830 when installed at Rome with his
mother, he had been affiliated to the Carbonari under the
influence of a young Milanese, Count Arese. A revolution
having broken out a little later at Bologna, he had hastened
there immediately to enrol himself in a troop of insurgents
who proposed nothing less than the overthrow of the
temporal power and the liberation of the Roman people.
His elder brother Charles Napoleon accompanied him. In
impetuous disorder the insurgents began to march on Rome.
At the first halt at Forli, Charles Napoleon was carried off
in two days by an eruptive fever. The revolutionary column,
however, pursued its way, crossed the Apennines and penetrated into Umbria. When it arrived before Spoleto, its
leaders learned that the Austrians were pursuing it with
forced marches ; in fact their advance guard was already
signalled. It became a question of immediate flight, and the
column was disbanded. Terrified at the idea of falling, like
his cousin the Duke of Reichstadt, into the clutches of
Metternich, Louis Napoleon came to a strange decision : he

went in search of the Archbishop of Spoleto, and asked for his help. The Prelate was touched by the plight of the young rebel. He gave him 5,000 frs., ordered him into a travelling-coach, and took him to a place of safety far from the Austrian bayonets. The name of the Archbishop was Mastaï-Ferretti, the future Pius IX.

Louis Napoleon always remembered with profound gratitude his benefactor of Spoleto, but the check to his enterprise did not in any way change the course of his ideas ; he remained the determined enemy of the Temporal Power and of the Papacy. Further, he was at this epoch more than irreligious, he was anti-religious : " Not only has the Prince no religion," says his tutor Vieillard, " but he hates religion and its ministers as much as a slave detests his chains and his oppressors."

Five years later, in New York, where he had taken refuge after the Strasbourg fiasco, he met a large group of Italian revolutionaries, who, harried by all the police in Europe, had come to seek an asylum in free America. Count Arese was among them. They formed there an ardent brotherhood, a little church which, like all churches, exalted and fortified itself by the sentiment of persecution.

Greeted with open arms, Louis Napoleon sought no other society than this. In their daily conversations they discussed in its every aspect and without ceasing the one subject : the resurrection of Italy by the abasement of Austria's power and by the abolition of the pontifical supremacy. Louis Napoleon approved of these ideas all the more since they fitted in so well with his dream of democratic Cæsarism, and he promised his companions in misfortune " that on the day when he should preside over the destinies of France he would support with all his strength the claims of Italian nationalism."

He did not fail, also, during the general elections of 1848, to recall in his manifestoes that he had been "a soldier of Roman independence in 1831."

The 25th December of the same year, two weeks after his accession to the Presidency of the Republic, saw the arrival at the Élysée of Count Arese, sent by the illustrious patriot Gioberti and the democratic ministers of Charles Albert officially to congratulate Louis Napoleon on his electoral triumph. This was, however, only a pretext. The former outlaw was charged in addition with a very secret mission : to solicit the energetic support of France for Piedmont in her preparations to reopen hostilities against Austria in revenge for her recent defeat at Custozza. Cordially received, Count Arese presented his request to the new chief of the French State, reminding him of their conversations in exile and calling to witness the solemn assurances given in New York. The Prince-President showed himself no less determined than formerly in the declaration of his sympathies for the Italian people, but he recalled to his questioner the embarrassments of his personal situation, the extreme reserve which was imposed upon him by the difficulties of politics at home and, above all, the reactionary passions of the Con-stitutional Assembly ; briefly, he declared that he was "powerless to do anything whatever in favour of Piedmont."

Count Arese was one of the most loyal men in the world and one of the most generous ; but he had a slow mind and a short-sighted point of view. He does not seem to have perceived the change which had taken place in the face, manners, gestures, and speech of his friend since their farewells on the banks of the Hudson. At that time Louis Napoleon had been ready-witted, communicative, ardent, capable even of terrible fits of passion ; now he was phlegmatic, taciturn, reticent, evasive, and masked. Experience of men and the test of adversity had taught him to conquer his nature, to control all his impulses, to be master of himself on all occasions. The companion of his childhood, Madame Cornu, gives us a striking example of this. She came to see him at the Élysée in December 1848 ; she had not seen him for a number of years, and found a face which she did not recognise, a strange face. " I asked him what he had in his eyes ? Nothing, he told me. The next day I saw him again and his eyes appeared to me still more strange. I perceived at last that he had learned to keep his eyelids half-closed and to assume an empty and dreamy expression."

Appalled by his diplomatic failure, and deceived in all his hopes, Count Arese returned to Turin carrying with him " the intimate conviction that on the day when Louis Napoleon is master of France and will no longer have to reckon with a conservative assembly, he will not forget his engagements of 1837." This conviction was not justified until ten years later, when Orsini was brutally to recall to the former conspirator of the Romagna his promise given in New York. In the meantime, three months after the mission of Arese to Paris, Field-Marshal Radetzky had full liberty to crush the army of Piedmont at Novara.

Without the patronage of the Catholics Louis Napoleon

could not have restored the Empire; without their co-
operation he could not have organised the new institutions
and have rooted them in the country. As in 1849, at the
time of the Roman Expedition, the effects of their close
alliance had not been slow in appearing. Benefits and
favours did not cease to flow upon the Church : restitution
of the Panthéon to its cult ; instructions to the prefects for
the observance of Sunday repose in Government offices ;
participation of the army in processions ; grants to sick
priests ; gifts to parishes ; favours to religious congregations ;
authorisation of provincial councils, which had been for-
bidden since 1624 ; attentions, favours, and all manner of
kindnesses towards the bishops : each day witnessed new
signs of the Imperial solicitude. The clergy on their side
were not sparing in their adulation of " the Constantine of
Christian France," the " Charlemagne of modern times."
Sometimes even they degenerated into base flattery which
did not fail to shock many of the faithful, especially among
the opponents of the Government. From his exile in
Belgium, General de Moricière could not contain his indignation : " The clergy believe that a charlatan, a crowned
impostor, can dispense them from converting souls. What
an error ! The clergy believe that the Carbonaro of yesterday
will become the sincere protector of Pius IX. What a
deplorable error ! . . . This man flatters the whole world to
reach his own ends, but his double nature is incompatible
with Catholic policy, which is eminently simple. The
coupling of the Faith with Freemasonry, of the Church with
the Revolution, is worse than frank impiety." The Comte
de Falloux, far from public life, retired in his manor-house

in Anjou, showed himself not less scandalised than La Moricière by " this infeoffment of Catholicism to the Empire," and he denounced its perils. " Believe me," he said one day to Veuillot ; " I know Louis Napoleon better than you. You can never expect from him a sincerely Catholic policy. His ideas on the Papacy are the ideas of his youth. When you have freed him from every rein, see where he will lead you. Do not prepare, therefore, so great a remorse for your conscience, so great a humiliation for your wisdom. Remain neutral ; that is the least you can do." But one might ask everything from the impetuous and virulent leader-writer of *L'Univers*, save to remain neutral. And daily he sang the praises of Cæsar, Constantine.

If Napoleon III rewarded the Catholics liberally for their co-operation, he understood well enough how to derive an immense profit from it ; for he had closely studied the tactics of the First Consul at the time of the Concordat. Then he conceived the novel design, borrowed also from the founder of the dynasty, to have himself consecrated by the Sovereign Pontiff in person at Notre-Dame in Paris. The negotiations were enveloped in profound mystery, one of those cloudy, tortuous mysteries so pleasing to the fancy of the conspirator. The bait was laid on the day after 2 December by a secret mission of General de Cotte to Rome, but it did not take substance until the month of October 1852, during the triumphal journey from Marseilles to Bordeaux, when in each town and through all the streets thousands of banners announced the Empire: *Ave, Cæsar Imperator !* . . . *Vox populi, vox Dei !* . . .

On 3 October at Carcassonne, the Prince-President had a long interview with the Bishop, Mgr de Bonnechose (who was later to receive the purple of the cardinalate when Archbishop of Rouen), and announced to him his intention of improving the status of the Catholic Church in France. Approaching the problem in its practical details, he declared himself ready to revise the organic Articles—that addition to the Concordat imposed by Bonaparte and which the Holy See had never ratified. He even added that he would willingly agree to " the modifications in the clauses of the Civil Code relative to marriage in order to bring them into harmony with the Canon Law of the Church and the prescriptions of the Council of Trent." He concluded by begging the Bishop to repeat his declarations to Pius IX.

Two months later, after being proclaimed Emperor, he chose as secret and permanent negotiator at Rome a young priest of distinguished address and great abilities who had just been nominated Auditor of the Rota at the Vatican, Mgr de Ségur. The theme which this ecclesiastic was charged to develop before the Pope may be summarised thus : Napoleon III could not conceive a higher thought or a more ardent desire than an intimate accord between Imperial France and the Apostolic stool. Nothing would contribute to this so much as the pontifical consecration at Notre Dame ; in the eyes of the world this would be the conclusive sign, the supreme symbol, the glorious seal of the alliance inaugurated between the Emperor of the French and the Vicar of Christ.

Pius IX had at first greeted these overtures with favour, for they laid bare a wonderful horizon before his acute mind.

Soon, however, the idea of going personally to Paris began to displease him. In conceding such a privilege to the youngest dynasty in Europe, a dynasty which was also very much suspect both in its origins and its principles, would he not be risking offending the old Catholic monarchs of Spain and of Austria? He had, therefore, invoked the example of Charlemagne to suggest to Napoleon III to come and receive the sacred unction at Rome. The proposition was at once so important and so new, that Mgr de Ségur had considered himself bound to confer directly with the Emperor, who received him at Saint-Cloud during the first days of July 1853. When the priest had finished pleading the cause confided to him by the Pope, Napoleon III replied that in theory he had no repugnance whatever to having himself consecrated, like Charlemagne, in the Vatican Church. "He added, however, in accents full of frankness and sincerity, that he had spent in Rome so unedifying a youth, which had left recollections of such a nature that he did not think it possible to present himself there again in so different a guise without giving rise to disagreeable reproaches and compromising the dignity of the consecration." In expressing himself in this manner the Emperor, perhaps, only obeyed the scruples of moral decency. In his fear of "compromising the dignity of the consecration" was there not already a certain presentiment of Orsini? Some months earlier, when talking with the secretary of his great friend Lord Malmesbury, he had said to him: "Italian revolutionaries are reduced politically to a powerless condition; the only one of their projects which disquiets me, the only one which would have a chance of succeeding, is assassination."

Pius IX, however, obsessed with his idea, insisted on the edifying example which Charlemagne had offered to the Christian world. " Let the Emperor Napoleon not hesitate, therefore, to repeat before the tomb of Saint Peter that beautiful act of penitence and humility. He gives as his objection the recollections of his impious youth : but why ? Since he affirms that he has abjured all that and is no longer the same man, let him prove it." At this moment the quarrel over the Holy Places set Europe aflame. On 5 January 1854 an Anglo-French fleet penetrated into the Black Sea ; on 27 March war was solemnly declared. Pius IX was then tempted to betake himself to Paris " to bless France while blessing the Emperor there." For had not this war, in fact, all the characteristics of a crusade in which Napoleon III was assuming the defence of Catholic interests in the East, and the protection of the Holy Sepulchre, against the intolerable encroachments of heretic Russia ? " Had he not also openly placed his squadrons under the patronage of the Holy Virgin and handed over the organisation of the military chaplaincies to the Jesuit Fathers ? " How could all these public acts of a piety so eloquent have failed to touch the affectionate heart of the Sovereign Pontiff ? How could they have failed to incline him " to hope for everything and to promise much ? "

While Mgr de Ségur was pursuing his secret negotiations with Rome, the Cabinets in Paris and Vienna were engaged in an official conversation which, in the secret recesses of Napoleon's mind, was indirectly connected with the negotiations for his consecration. Since his coronation, and especially since his marriage, the Emperor had his eyes

turned continually to Austria. He felt himself a parvenu in
old monarchical Europe and, too often, he perceived that
the great Courts did not receive him without a certain hauteur.
In this connection the Empress Eugénie showed herself the
more sensitive as she had developed an ardent admiration for
Marie Antoinette. She was fervently collecting objects which
had belonged to the martyred Queen, furniture, pictures,
statuettes, portraits, books, jewels, ornaments, fans, and lace.
It became a passion with her, a cult, a sort of fetish. She
had taken to herself somewhat ingeniously the illusion of
belonging to the privileged caste of the old sovereign families.
As to the Emperor, what attracted him towards Austria was
the thought that an alliance with the illustrious house of
Habsburg would greatly add to his power.

Persigny desired this alliance no less than Napoleon, for
he saw in it, above all, a check on the Utopian imagination of
his master, a guarantee of balance and of wisdom for French
policy. He even recapitulated in an ingenious formula the
mutual advantages which would be assured to the two Allies
when he said to Baron von Hübner, the ambassador of
Francis Joseph, " The Emperor Napoleon has the masses on
his side and Austria has the upper classes on her side. Give
us the upper classes and we will give you the masses." The
ambassador, however, was under no illusion as to the true
motives of Napoleon's idea, for he added in his diary :
" These words of Persigny betray the intimate suffering of
the Tuileries ; they feel themselves disdained by the old
Courts of the continent. That is the worm that gnaws the
Emperor Napoleon."

In Vienna the idea of an alliance with the restorer of the

7

French Empire, with the sovereign who had dared to take
the name of Napoleon III, as if the Duke of Reichstadt had
really reigned, met with no favour. His former relations
with the Italian revolutionaries were too well known; the
requisition directed against him in 1831 by the Imperial
Public Prosecutor in Milan, accusing him of " occupying a
high rank among the Carbonari," was especially remembered,
as were also the foolish hopes which Piedmont had placed in
him on the eve of Novara. In addition to this, and in spite
of the monarchical title of which he had taken possession, in
spite of the conservative principles which he had solemnly
declared since the beginning of his reign, Vienna saw in him
nothing but a Cæsarian adventurer, a dangerous idealogue, as
devoid of scruples as he was of good sense, and capable of
the worst extravagancies. Never—it was said at the Hofburg
—will he leave Europe to sleep in peace.

The war in the East had soon confirmed this prophecy.
At the outset Austria had no intention of acting otherwise
than as a neutral in the conflict, but in the course of events,
from the prolongation of hostilities, finally and especially
from the unforeseen death of the Emperor Nicholas, she
had been led to adopt a menacing attitude towards Russia.
On 15 March 1855 Austria invited the plenipotentiaries of
the belligerent Powers to meet at Vienna to obtain the
reluctant consent of the Russian Government to make the
great sacrifices which already appeared to be an inevitable
condition of peace. Foreseeing the ill-success that attended
these negotiations, France and England used every effort to
hasten on the hour when the Austrian army would be morally
obliged to take part in the conflict.

The question was one of so high an importance that the French Minister for Foreign Affairs, Drouyn de Lhuys, had resolved to take part in person in the deliberations in the Ballplatz. Received in audience on his arrival by Francis Joseph, he said: "What brings me to Your Majesty far more than the desire of making peace with Russia is that of concluding and making effective an alliance with Austria." The task which he thus allotted himself was a difficult and a dangerous one, so great was the mistrust inspired by the policy of the Tuileries in every circle at Vienna. Diplomat of the best school as he was, thoroughly trained in the tactics of his profession, and full of resource, he soon turned the situation to account. After a month of clever effort he seemed to be reaching his goal when suddenly Napoleon III recalled him to Paris, and disavowed him. On 8 May, when offering his resignation to the Emperor, he wrote to him in the grip of a sinister presentiment: "Your Majesty has told me that you persist in rejecting the proposals of Austria. *In my eyes, however, such a rejection is the first step in a fatal policy*. Let Heaven guide you, Sire, and protect you in the way which you have chosen." On learning of the retirement of the Minister, the Director of Political Affairs at the Quai d'Orsay, Thouvenel, who could not but know all the undercurrents, wrote with truth to his friend Bénédetti: "You see that our general policy is on the point of going off the rails." It was not only going off the rails in the direction of Vienna: it was going off the rails also in the direction of Rome. It is, perhaps, the second derailment which explains the abruptness of the first.

The great affair of the pontifical consecration had miscarried. After many interludes and adjournments, it really seemed to be on the verge of conclusion. Hence Napoleon III at last found it necessary to reveal to his intimate councillors and certain legal authorities the modifications which he was preparing to introduce into the administration of Catholic affairs in accordance with the wishes of the Vatican. All those whom he had taken into his confidence, Persigny, Troplong, Portalis, Billault, Delangle, Dupin, had shown him in a more or less marked form their surprise and their disapproval. " What," they said to him, " is the Emperor about to destroy with his own hands the basis of the Concordat, that masterpiece of the First Consul ! Had he reflected on the discontent which this innovation could not fail to arouse in French consciences, which were at all times so rebellious against ultramontane pretensions ? " They also represented to him that after two or three years of his reign the ceremony of the consecration would appear somewhat tardy, that it would offer rather too easy a theme for the sarcasm of the opposition parties. They finally asked him if he did not fear that in inviting Pius IX to Paris he would subjugate himself irrevocably to the Vatican and the French clericals.

Among all these strong arguments the last seems to have touched Napoleon III more than the others. The bishops had already frequently harassed him by the exaggeration and the obsequiousness of their panegyrics, of which one had drawn from Falloux this irritated epigram : " These are the people who are raising the beauty of the Empress to the height of an imperial institution." In multiplying itself this displeasing impression had little by little revived in the Emperor's mind his former distrust of the priests. As in the days of his free-thinking youth, he said one day to Persigny: "The black men disgust me." The charm was broken. Meanwhile Mgr de Ségur, who suffered from a disease of the eyes, had become suddenly blind; and the physical disability of the negotiator accomplished the final ruin of the negotiations themselves.

To all appearance the relations of Napoleon III and the Church remained entirely unchanged; nothing was altered in their attitudes and official speeches. Only a few acute observers were soon to discover in the spirit of the sovereign the signs of underlying conversion. It was Veuillot who perceived it first. Thereupon, full of bitterness, he cried: "Decidedly Napoleon III is nothing more than a perfected Louis Philippe." Before long Mgr de Bonnechose, who had lately been transferred from Carcassonne to Évreux, became disquieted by the new tendencies which he thought he could discern in the Imperial policy, and when he was received in audience by the Emperor on 10 February 1857, he solemnly declared "that God would abandon his cause if he himself abandoned the cause of God."

V

To what extent had Cavour read the silent vacillations in Napoleon's mind? It cannot be doubted that he already had a clear and complete comprehension of them when he left Paris on 27 April 1856. If not, how can it be explained that on his return to Turin he had given to Piedmontese policy towards Austria a determinedly aggressive character ? All that he had observed during the Congress, all that his quick little ferret's eyes had been able to observe here and there, especially his own piercing glance into the dark soul of Napoleon III, had aroused in him the conviction that the Elect of the French would henceforth proceed without halting along the way of adventure ; that he would always be led by his natural tendencies, by his dreamy ideology, by his Messianic conception of the Imperial power, and that sooner or later he would certainly make war on Austria. Apart from this conviction, he carried away from his interviews with Lord Clarendon the impression that the cause of Italian Independence would have the right to count, should occasion arise, on the sympathy of the English people, if not on the moral support of the British Government itself.

Finally, in his frank conversations with Count Orloff, he had touched the festering sore, " the fierce bitterness " which the crafty hostility of Austria during the Crimean War had left in the heart of Russia ; and he had immediately perceived the profit that later he might draw from it.

Thus, piece by piece, all the mechanism of a great diplomatic action was discovered to his mind.

CHAPTER IV

ORSINI

CHAPTER IV

ORSINI

I

CLEARLY perceiving the task that lay ahead of him, and being conscious, even to his inmost being, of a new access of strength, Cavour immediately set to work. An urgent and preliminary duty awaited him on his return to Turin. Desiring to hold all the reins of government in his own hands, he found himself embarrassed and hindered in his work by an inefficient colleague, Luigi Cibrario, to whom he had given the portfolio of Foreign Affairs. Hence his first step was to remove Cibrario from his post and to take upon himself its duties, without relinquishing the Ministry of Finance. On the day following that on which he took this step (6 May) he was questioned in Parliament as to the relations between Austria and Piedmont. Thus afforded a pretext for doing so, he coldly declared that " the two countries are further than ever from understanding one another, for the principles by which they are inspired are irreconcilable." Speaking of the Congress of Paris, and the part taken in its deliberations by the Piedmontese delegation, he gave utterance to the ominous words : " For the first time in our history the Italian Question has been discussed in a European Congress, not as at Verona and Laibach for the purpose of adding to the woes of Italy by

riveting fresh chains upon her, but with the exalted object
of seeking to put an end to her misfortunes, of proclaiming
openly the sympathy in which she is held by the Great
Powers.　Her case has come before the tribunal of public
opinion, to which, as the Emperor of the French has said
in a memorable phrase, belongs the right of final judgment,
the ultimate victory.　The process may well be long-drawn-
out, and many vicissitudes of fortune may be experienced
in its course.　Nevertheless, confident in the justice of our
cause, we await the verdict with equanimity."　All veils
were thus torn away.　Europe continued to meet in Paris
for barely another fortnight.　Even Napoleon III, when
he said, " peace would not last for long," did not contemplate
that its duration would prove so brief.　With Cavour,
however, events moved apace.　Swiftly he reached the
climax of the drama, *in medias res*.

At this critical hour, with his boats already burned behind
him, what was the plan of campaign he had sketched out ?
It is precisely in this decisive moment of his career that he
showed himself, in his grasp of the essential factors in the
situation, a statesman of the order of Richelieu and Cromwell,
of Chatham, Stein, and Bismarck.　Rarely do statesmen
see clearly the supreme interest of their country, the turning-
point in its time of tribulation, the summons to its historic
mission to devote its energies, ambitions, and aspirations
to a well-defined and determinate aim.　Rarer still than the
ability to frame a great idea is the ability to perceive at the
same time the means of giving effect to it ; to visualise the
road along which to travel ; to estimate accurately the
strength of opposing and supporting forces ; to give con-

sistent expression to the idea ; to accept in advance, even to
create on occasion, all the conditions necessary to its success.
Finally, when the battle is at last joined, to act upon the spur
of the moment and to keep strategical plans within the limits
set by the extent of available resources.

Of the truth of one political axiom above all others
Cavour was profoundly convinced : that the strength of a
nation consists in the synthesis and correlation of all its vital
forces : that the separation of internal from external policy
is in the nature of a governmental expedient, more apparent
than real, and that all the devices and groupings of skilful
diplomacy are worthless unless they have behind them the
support of a strong army, prosperous finances, good administration, and national discipline of mind and of body. When
in the spring of 1856 the curtain rose on the first act of the
drama of the *Risorgimento*, Cavour's spirited and clear
imagination revealed to him the existence of two tasks of
equal importance and urgency, the one embracing the whole
field of home politics, the other presenting the spectacle of
one of the most difficult problems ever posed for diplomatic
ingenuity to solve.

At home his task amounted to no less than that of placing
tiny Piedmont in such a state of internal prosperity and
strength that she would be able to take upon herself, in the
name of all Italy, the battle for national existence. In pursuit
of this task Cavour's creative and reforming ability left
untouched no single department of public life. Finance,
customs, commerce, agriculture, public works, industry,
ports, railways, military training and supplies, fortifications
——he handled them one and all with an all-embracing

capacity, a breadth of view, a fertility of resource, a burning and contagious enthusiasm that found in this wealth of opportunities ample scope for the employment of those talents for organisation and management which he had developed during his twenty years' apprenticeship at Léri. It would be tedious even to summarise the full extent of his activities. How he laboured to increase the national revenue and decrease the national debt, to reform abuses in the administration, to increase and perfect the strength of the artillery, to create a naval arsenal at Spezia, to strengthen the fortifications of Casale and Alessandria, to tunnel through Mont Cenis, to augment the prosperity of Genoa as a port, to improve the navigation of the Po——inspiring everything, organising everything, superintending everything.

For, in truth, he was a dictator. But his dictatorship partook of a singular—not to say paradoxical—nature in that it was exercised through persuasion, and with the most complete regard for constitutional forms, and in strict accord with liberal principles; he never either sought or used a method other than that of public discussion under the authority of Parliament. Hence his was not an autocratic dictatorship; it was, on the contrary, a parliamentary dictatorship. Cavour, indeed, was, and throughout his life he remained, a convinced Liberal after the English pattern. He loved liberty for itself with a love free from any doctrinaire systems or sentimental dreams; nor was he under any illusion as to its dangers and inconveniences. Nevertheless, he saw in it the best guarantee for the public weal. He thought that in opposition and criticism were to be found the mainsprings of good government, and, with John Stuart Mill, he believed that the invaluable and necessary function of a Parliament was " to give a nation an outlet for grievances and opinions." Moreover, he found justification for his belief in the lively debates that took place in the Carignan Palace ; there his opponents were in the fortunate position of being able to criticise his policy and its cost to the national exchequer, while Cavour could not at that time give any public indication of the aim he was pursuing. Yet he never refused their challenge, and invariably and readily mounted the tribune without showing the least traces of annoyance.

He has himself revealed the philosophy that animated his conduct. One day someone in seeking to please him said : " Ah ! your task would be much easier under an absolutist regime." Cavour replied angrily : " You forget that under an absolutist regime I would not wish to be a minister, and, above all, that I would have no chance of becoming one. I am what I am because I have the opportunity of being a constitutional minister. . . . Parliamentary government has its inconveniences, as have all governments ; nevertheless it is the best. I confess myself impatient of a certain kind of opposition, and this I combat with vigour. Yet when I reflect upon it, I am always glad that I have to fight it because it compels me to explain my ideas to the best of my ability, to redouble my efforts to win over public opinion. An autocratic minister commands. A minister under a constitutional government has to persuade and convince in order to be obeyed. I am sure that I am right. Believe me, the worst of parliaments is preferable to the best of anterooms." Cavour was no less a Royalist because he was a Liberal. He could not conceive of liberty except within the framework of a constitutional monarchy. It was not that he abhorred republicanism in principle; rather that he thought it incapable of safeguarding the permanent interests of the State and the normal working of free institutions. "A form of republicanism, suited to our needs, our customs, and to the general state of Europe, has yet to be discovered."

Then, too, he was completely devoted to Victor Emmanuel, the *Re Galantuomo*, who had distinguished himself by his scrupulous observance of constitutional practices, in marked contrast to those other Italian princes of his day, and even to the Sovereign Pontiff himself, who perjured themselves in the eyes of their subjects. But another and still more cogent reason attached Cavour to his King. The flag of Italian independence had been entrusted to the ancient House of Savoy and it was to Victor Emmanuel before all others that Italian patriots looked as to a leader. As early as May 1856 Cavour had written to one of his friends who was a priest in Florence : "Providence has imposed upon Piedmont the task of fighting with all its strength for the liberation of the Peninsula. I tell you that neither King Victor Emmanuel nor his people will fail in this duty." In pouring out his heart to another friend in Florence he wrote about this time : "Henceforth we must be the protagonists of the Italian cause on the battlefield, in diplomatic congresses, and before the tribunal of the public opinion of Europe." Every word in these two letters could have been written by Victor Emmanuel.

II

Although the King and his Minister were thus in accord on the object of their policy, it would be an error to suppose that their daily intercourse was free from discord. The two men were too dissimilar in character, education, and in their methods of thought. Victor Emmanuel was a man of rough, even vulgar, tastes, but of a noble and chivalrous spirit. Cavour, despite his bourgeois appearance, possessed cultivated manners and tastes.

Surly of speech, untidy in his dress, the King hated nothing more than the *salons* where he invariably scandalised the fashionable world by the coarseness of his conversation. For dinner, he liked great dishes of steaming ragouts, beloved of the common people, of which the arrival at the table was announced beforehand by the smell of hot onions and garlic. He cut down the Court ceremonies, the receptions and levees, to the minimum. Now and then, however, he was forced to give a ceremonial banquet. On such an occasion he would not even unfold his napkin, and steadfastly refused all the dishes——too insipid and refined for his coarse taste——which were offered to him. With his sword between his legs, his strong hands folded one above the other across the hilt, he sat and watched his guests without troubling to conceal from them his boredom and his impatience.

One characteristic Victor Emmanuel shared with Cavour, a characteristic as strongly marked in the one as in the other : love of country life. For the King, however, this also meant an opportunity for escaping from the restraints of the City and Court, and for satisfying his exuberant vitality in bodily exercise. On his country estate of La Mandria, situated less than an hour's journey from Turin, in the midst of woods, he gave himself up untiringly to his favourite pastime—horsemanship. Accustomed from his infancy to horses, he had learned to understand them as few others did. Although he sat a horse badly, he rode well in a stolid and unshakable manner that revealed itself in the nervous clutch of his enormous legs upon the horse's flanks. As a matter of course he preferred restive animals for the pure pleasure of fighting with them and mastering them. After horsemanship, hunting was his favourite occupation. Not hunting in the peaceful and game-haunted plains in which Cavour walked at Léri, but among the rugged precipices of the Alps that overhung the valleys of Grisanche, d'Aosta, and Locana. An attaché of the French Legation at Turin, named d'Ideville, has described with a wealth of picturesque detail Victor Emmanuel in his familiar character of Alpine hunter. " Frequently, towards the end of autumn, or even during the winter, he goes away with two aides-de-camp to hunt chamois in the mountains. There, dressed in a shirt, rifle in hand, he hastens over the rocks, followed by a number of hardy peasants. Often he sleeps in the open and eats in a cottage, if one can be found. Then, alert and well, he returns to Turin, while his unhappy aides-de-camp almost invariably come back ill or worn out." With so great a capacity and need for physical exercise, it is not surprising that the King hated governmental work with its routine of reports, dispatches, and calculations. Besides, as his education had been much neglected, he always had a horror of books. He used to amuse himself by saying : " *I am not a scholar*." To a secretary who brought him a pile of papers, Victor Emmanuel exclaimed : " Don't worry me ! I did not become King to be at everybody's beck and call ! " In this more than in any other respect he differed from Cavour, who was a glutton for work. Summer and winter, from five in the morning until eleven at night, he read, wrote, studied, and took part in conferences ; equalling if not surpassing, in his general knowledge as in the width, depth, and keenness of his intellect, the leading statesmen of his day.

Victor Emmanuel was too clever not to recognise the genius of Cavour and, although in his presence he felt himself awkward and an inferior, he yet tolerated Cavour on that account. Often, in a Council, he was forced to abandon his most cherished ideas because he lacked the ability to defend them. Further, the King, who had the frank, open, and simple nature of the soldier, instinctively disliked the dialectics of Cavour, who beneath an apparently frank exterior concealed an astute and malicious nature, and who never hesitated to use whatever expedient or subterfuge occurred to him, or, in the words of the spirited d'Azeglio, to keep a card up his sleeve. Hence, in spite of a long and intimate collaboration in the service of a great cause, neither sympathy nor friendship ever existed between Victor Emmanuel and Cavour.

Cavour and Victor Emmanuel call to mind Louis XIII and Richelieu. The comparison, indeed, is not a wholly just one. For the great Cardinal was rewarded not only by Louis's confidence and respect but also by his close and constant friendship. Over two hundred letters in the royal holograph destroy beyond resurrection the legend that represented Richelieu as a tyrant, imposing his will upon

8

the King, and Louis XIII as a weak monarch resigning
himself, with death in his soul, to an execrated domination.
If the legend be revived in order that it may be applied to
the relations between Victor Emmanuel and Cavour, docu-
mentary evidence will be readily forthcoming to prove its
falsity, though in this case the evidence will be less con-
vincing.

One of the most embittered quarrels between Victor
Emmanuel, the son of the pious Charles Albert, and Cavour
was occasioned by the great religious conflict that raged in
Piedmont.   For six years the Catholic Church in Piedmont
had been put to a severe test.   Civil immunity of the clergy,
ecclesiastical courts, right of asylum, the magnificent revenue
of the bishops and monasteries—all these survivals of a
former age had been abolished or condemned.   Moreover,
in this battle, Cavour had not hesitated to be a leader.
Tolerant upon matters of dogma, he retained little trace of
the beliefs he had been taught in infancy, although he continued to have a respect for religion as such, a vague sympathy
for Catholic ritual, and a superstitious fear of what lay beyond
the veil.   The saying of Chamfort about the Duc de Créqui
might be applied to Cavour : " He did not believe in God,
but he feared God."   Hence no conscientious scruples
troubled his championship of the rights of the laity against
sacerdotal pretensions ; of the separation of the temporal
from the spiritual power in the State.   Nor were any such
scruples present when he sought to realise his dream, which
in those days seemed a heresy : " A free Church in a free
State."   But, above all, in devoting all his energy and
will-power to the service of this idea, Cavour had in mind

an interest greater than the welfare of Piedmont : the national cause of Italy.

These sacrilegious and destructive laws against the Piedmontese clergy were anathema to Rome, and there was talk of recalling the Nuncio from Turin. Cavour was not disposed to avert this alarming rupture ; in his heart of hearts he even desired it. The melancholy outcome of the Roman crisis of 1848, the disaster that overtook the Guelf adventure, the Pope's departure, and his retraction, greatly troubled him. He had immediately drawn from these occurrences a number of conclusions, arbitrary and of importance for the future : this Papacy, described by the monk Tosti as " the Sacred Ark of Italy," would always be his bitterest enemy ; the *Risorgimento* of the Peninsula would have to resist the Papacy, otherwise the movement would utterly fail ; the destruction of the temporal power was a necessary condition of Italian independence and unity ; " Pius IX and Italy " was no longer true, but " Pius IX or Italy " : " for no agreement of any kind between Piedmont and the Holy See is either desirable or possible."

Victor Emmanuel, a sincere Christian and a rigorous observer of forms and ceremonies, was greatly distressed by this radical and trenchant policy. Besides, he was still obedient to the influence of his old tutor, Mgr Charvaz, now Archbishop of Genoa. Finally, he had both affection and reverence for Pius IX, who, always squeamish over liberal initiative, had fled for refuge to the highest peaks of theology, and was deeply engaged in admitting the exemption from original sin of the Mother of the Word Incarnate, and in defining the high privileges of the Immaculate Conception.

Cavour, therefore, had the greatest difficulty in obtaining the King's sanction for the provocative measures continually dictated by his national anti-clericalism. But he remained at the King's side, and allowed no outburst on his part. One day, when the sovereign's patience had been too severely tried, it was noticed that he was " ghastly pale and bowed down with so great a weight of sorrow, that he was pitiable." On another occasion, 1 August 1856, Cavour, who had gone to recuperate at Baveno on Lake Maggiore, wrote to the Home Secretary, Rattazzi : " For Heaven's sake be firm with the King ; tell him that once he comes into direct contact with Rome, he will raze to the ground that edifice we have been building with infinite pains for the last eight years. It is impossible for us to preserve our influence in Italy if we treat with the Pope. We cannot push things too far ; but at the same time we cannot retreat even a foot ! You know that I am no ' priestophobe,' that I shall voluntarily extend the liberties the Church enjoys. But in present circumstances a reconciliation with the Holy See would inevitably prejudice us. If necessary, then, *frighten the King* and on no account allow him to hold converse with Rome."

There was, it seems, one subject upon which Victor Emmanuel and Cavour thoroughly understood each other, upon which, at least, no conflict was possible between them. That subject was Women.

It was not that they subscribed to the same creed. Cavour's affections were by no means platonic, but his sensual imagination, though ardent and imperious, could not comprehend love without that intoxication of the heart, that romantic play, without all that Benjamin Constant meant by "tender nonsense." The King, on the contrary, was deplorably vulgar in his passions.

Married to an Austrian Archduchess, Maria Adelaide, a delightful, visionary creature destined for an early grave, Victor Emmanuel continually betrayed her by short liaisons or sudden follies. He finally became enamoured, while his wife was still alive, of the daughter of a drum-major, a beautiful wanton, tall, high-coloured, lively, and muscular, Rosine by name. She was only sixteen when the King placed himself at her feet. Artful, and rather sly than intelligent, she very quickly made a captive of her lover, and amused him by the audacity of her language and the coarseness of her actions. Victor Emmanuel installed her at Mandria, unhappy unless he were near her; for in their daily intimacy he could at last satisfy to the full his detestation of good manners and of etiquette, his taste for independence, for unceremoniousness, and for licentiousness. Their intimacy was not undisturbed by storms. Rosine sometimes flew into a rage with him and, her innate coarseness all unbridled, made terrible scenes. She did not consider herself bound to be faithful to him, and among her casual lovers was to be found a rich jeweller of Turin.

Shortly after Maria Adelaide's death it began to be whispered at Court that the King was bent upon ennobling the drum-major's daughter under the title of Countess Mirafiori, and upon legitimising her children. It was even said that he wished to marry her, and a glance at Rosine's figure left little doubt that the event was at hand.

Then Cavour intervened. Using the bold language Sully

had used when he showed Henry IV that he had no right to marry Gabrielle d'Estrées, Cavour conjured Victor Emmanuel to relinquish his plan, the carrying out of which would be an evil omen for the success of the task upon which the nation was engaged. A violent scene took place between the two men. One of the few persons to whom the details were known said that " on this occasion Cavour's boldness was prodigious and almost amounted to a grave scandal." The King finally bowed to the high interests that were at stake. Several days later, unbosoming himself to one of his intimate friends, he expressed himself in words still informed by his anger: " My position alone prevents me from demanding satisfaction of Cavour; this is one of those affairs that should be settled by cold steel; but I must consider the country " (*La mia sola posizione m'impedi allora di chiedere ragione a Cavour; furono cose dal coltello; ma devo pensare al paese*).

If Cavour made too much of this matrimonial incident, it was because he risked the ruin at a critical moment of one of the most intricate tasks he had ever undertaken.

III

Passing through Turin during the Crimean War, Justus Liebig, the famous German chemist, noticed the intensity of national feeling there displayed, and summed it up: " This little country at the foot of the Alps has strength enough to vanquish death and to carry the torch of life through the whole Peninsula." This was Cavour's belief expressed in so many words.

It was not enough, however, that Piedmont should inspire the nation's striving after freedom; that it had the right to pose before the world as protagonist and plenipotentiary of Italy; that the House of Savoy was able to fulfil its mission of leader as it alone could: it was imperative to rally all Italian patriots round Victor Emmanuel.

A large number of these patriots—and among them a number of notable and conspicuous persons—were ardent republicans who had hitched their wagon to the star of popular insurrection, believing that it alone should lead Italy. Cavour was not one to be caught by words; he went beneath them to the roots of things. " Popular insurrection " to him meant disorder, disintegration, anarchy; briefly, that disastrous impotence that had characterised all Italian insurrections since 1815. What was the problem exactly? It was to expel Austria. Bands of insurgents would never succeed in expelling Austria, one of the greatest diplomatic and military powers in Europe; alliances and armies were necessary for its accomplishment. The Savoy dynasty alone was in a position to procure either. The republicans would have to be weaned from their sects, from their unfruitful Utopian dreams, from their antiquated taste for revolutionary practices and plots; they would have to be enrolled in the nation's service under a monarchical flag. Those who could not be so converted would have to be removed to where they could do no mischief.

This taming of the republican party was one of the most thankless tasks Cavour had ever set himself, and, consequently, the one at which his capacities for contriving, adjusting, managing, and wearing down were seen at their beſt. Mirabeau's happy conceit, "political dispensary," uttered after reading Machiavelli, exactly describes Cavour's activities. The "dispenser" did not rely on dexterity alone; he had courage. None of his predecessors had dared to ſtretch out a hand to the revolutionaries and solicit their co-operation. Count Balbo and Chevalier d'Azeglio, ardent Nationaliſts as they were, had shrunk from the depravity of such an act. Had Cavour been a man to explain his acts, he could have taken refuge behind a great monarchical authority. On 18 July 1814 Joseph de Maiſtre wrote from St. Petersburg to the Miniſter for Foreign Affairs of Victor Emmanuel I : " Watch the Italian spirit born of the Revolution. Our neutral policy, timid and fumbling, is fatal in the present circumſtances. The King should place himself at the head of the Italians; in the whole civil and military services not a single place, even at Court, is given to the Revolutionaries ! It's a vitally important thing, essential, necessary—words fail me ! " The writer of this letter had already said : " The whole art of a ſtatesman is *to know how to work with Fate.*"

Skilful though Cavour was, there was one revolutionary whom he tried in vain to tame, and, unfortunately, he was the moſt dangerous one of all : Mazzini.

This little, sickly man, greenish of complexion, black of hair, with a vaſt brow, blue eyes that ſtabbed and blazed, was an apoſtle, a fanatic, a visionary. His motto was " God and the People." His programme was as laconic : " Italy one and republican, Rome at her head." It might almoſt be said that the vision of the Eternal City shone upon all his

MAZZINI.

flights of fancy. "Rome is ours: God and men declare it. From Rome we have inherited the language that binds us in brotherhood. In Rome our history began and continues. A thousand years of great memories have anointed the mother of Italy and the heart of our national unity. From Rome we have twice ruled the world. Twice from her walls has been breathed the mighty breath that imposed a common civilisation upon the world. After the Rome of the Cæsars, after the Rome of the Popes, the Rome of the People! . . ." Such language from his lips was something more than mere religious rhetoric; it was an express revelation, an actual manifestation, that had been vouchsafed him " during the course of a terrible moral temptation " one evening in the prison at Savone, where he was serving his hard apprenticeship to prison life. That evening he had felt the breath of Ezekiel and Isaiah upon his face. Since then he had never doubted his high calling nor ceased to believe in his own infallibility. In this experience may be found the origin of his imperious despotism, his trenchant ironies, and the storm of fury that swept over him at the least contradiction. Withdrawn from the world, sustained by his passions and his dreams, he made of every fact an abstract idea. Experience counted for nothing in his eyes. Twenty years of successive defeats in Piedmont, in Savoy, in Lombardy, in Calabria, and in the Marches, at Rome, at Naples, and in Sicily, entailing as they did upon thousands the scaffold, the hulks, proscription, misery, ruin, evils without number—these had taught him nothing. Disillusionment never came to shatter his hopes. Gloomy and romantic, he was never happy unless engaged in secret machinations, conspiracies, and crimes. If he personally was not a regicide, he had at any rate justified regicide. "Nations sometimes go through exceptional periods when nothing can be judged according to normal standards; during these periods the individual must be guided by God and his conscience alone. The sword that in Judith's hand severed the head of Holofernes was sacred; sacred was the dagger of Brutus; sacred the stiletto that gave the signal for the Sicilian Vespers."

All his life Mazzini was obviously trembling on the brink of insanity. He displayed all the symptoms of that formidable psychosis that inspires great fanatics, great redressers of wrong, great lovers of justice: belief in a supernatural calling, immeasurable pride, irritability of temper, gloomy spirits, enduring passion, arrogant talk upon one unending, unalterable subject, dogmatism in argument, and an absolute indifference to facts. Mutual understanding and friendship were an impossibility between such a man and Cavour: their minds worked in contrary directions. Cavour indeed did not waste his time in negotiating with this incorrigible conspirator. He contented himself with placing Mazzini under police surveillance in his several cities of refuge— London, Zurich, Lausanne. If Mazzini had sought to enter Piedmont with the outbreak of the war for national existence, Cavour would have had him shot like a dog.

All Italian republicans were not utopists and madmen, however, and four men in particular attracted Cavour's attention: Daniel Manin, the heroic defender of revolted Venice; the Marquis Pallavicino-Trivulzio, a Lombard patriot of ancient lineage who had been nineteen years incarcerated in Spielberg; Giuseppe La Farina, a Sicilian agitator, scrupulous and broad-minded; and Garibaldi, demagogue of Nice, ex-corsair in the revolted fleet of Brazil and General at the service of the Roman Republic, a man in whom seemed to live again all the energy, all the daring, all the wiles, of the most famous *condottieri*. Cavour determined to appeal to the patriotism of these four men; to prove to them that Italy's enfranchisement was not to be won by catchwords and conspiracies, but by alliances and armies; to persuade them to sacrifice their individual dreams on the altar of their country's highest interest; through them to guide the torrential streams of revolution into the great national river. He chose La Farina, then in Turin, as spokesman and principal advocate of his scheme.

Negotiations began on 12 September 1856 between the Piedmontese statesman and the Sicilian agitator. Cavour had arranged to give audience to La Farina at 6 o'clock in the morning, the time of day Cavour preferred for personal interviews. This early hour suited him, for he rose at 4 o'clock. The conference was free from restraint, worthy of the gravity of its occasion. Cavour was impelled to lay all his cards on the table, and to speak particularly of one of the objectives the republicans had most at heart: the political and moral unity of the future Italy, the absolute equality and the intimate blending of all the Italian elements within the reconstituted nation. But Cavour had not the entire confidence of his four chosen men upon this fundamental principle of their programme. They suspected him of using the *Risorgimento* as a means to an end, and that end the preferment of Piedmont, the substituting of a Piedmontese for an Austrian hegemony in the Peninsula—the " Pied-montising " of Italy. That they could never agree to. " I hold Piedmontism," wrote Pallavicino, " to be our most formidable foe."

Cavour gave his early-morning visitor every assurance. " I am persuaded," he said, " that Italy will become one united State, with Rome its capital." He closed the interview with the words : " Come to see me as often as you wish. But I may not forget that I am the King's Minister and that I have no right to compromise the dynasty. So always come in the morning, soon after dawn ; without anyone knowing that you come, without anyone seeing you, so that if I am questioned in Parliament or by diplomats, like St. Peter I can deny you, saying ' I do not know this man.' "

Conducted with the same cordiality, the conferences that followed soon engendered an agreement over principles that immediately took shape in a National Italian Society under the presidency of the Marquis Pallavicino and the vice-presidency of Garibaldi. It was a bizarre and hybrid association, adapting itself quite remarkably to circumstances. In Piedmont, for instance, it enjoyed legal protection and official indulgence, while in the other Italian States it was a secret organisation. Extending its ramifications gradually over the whole of Italy ; preparing hot-beds of propaganda and rallying centres ; recruiting trained men by the thousand without distinction of class or party ; finding out the brains in the army, in the police, at Court, and even in the princely families it hated ; undermining in advance all parts of the doomed edifice—in Cavour's hands this machine became the most powerful of weapons, the most useful of tools, for the demolition that was preparing.

IV

Cavour had not expected that all these fine results of internal policy would smooth away the friction in the diplomatic relations between Piedmont and Austria; on the contrary, day by day the irritation grew. Incidents, trifling at first, continually arose, and soon the duel between Turin and Vienna was uninterrupted. Cavour displayed an astonishing adroitness of attack, of thrust and thrust again, of re-attack, sometimes putting Count Buol, his adversary, with whom he had already crossed swords at the Congress of Paris, completely out of countenance. Cavour's skill in aggression might justly be compared to the rapid, tormenting, and infuriating manœuvres of picadors and banderillos at a bull-fight.

Vienna was scandalised. Old Prince Metternich, pontiff and law-giver of the ancient European order, the statesman who in 1815 had thought to have stifled Italian nationality for ever in the grave, an old man who had only another three years to live, nearly choked with indignation. " I already number myself among the dead," he wrote to Buol, " but my nerves still vibrate to certain galvanic shocks. Well, one of these shocks is the stand taken by the Court at Turin. Never was followed a policy more despicable and false ; never was there a labyrinth of iniquity and insolent calumnies so calculated to lead one astray." The illustrious old man was not yet at the end of his troubles ; the " galvanic vibrations " of his nerves ceased only with his breath.

One day the Turin Cabinet, openly engaged in developing its military power, ordered the strengthening of the works at Alessandria, and authorised a public assessment for the purchase of one hundred cannon. This afforded Cavour the pretext for speaking before the Chamber as if Piedmont were the appointed defender of Italy against the Habsburgs. Nothing more irritated the proud Viennese Court than this claim of the little sub-Alpine kingdom to set itself up as the champion of Italy against Austria. Added to this, all the Italian princes, the Dukes of Parma and Modena, the Grand Duke of Tuscany, the King of Naples, clamoured round Francis Joseph, conjuring him " to bridle the arrogance of Piedmont." Cavour, needless to say, met the remonstrances laid before him by Count Paar, the Austrian Minister, with great coldness. His own personal feelings are clearly shown in this letter to his friend General Dabormida, who was then in London : " Don't hasten your return. See Palmerston, see Clarendon. Give Clarendon my very kindest remembrances. Assure him that we shall do nothing foolish. But add that if Austria provokes us beyond endurance, if she forces on us the choice between dishonour and war, we shall choose, war." Counsels of moderation prevailed at the Ballplatz, and the affair settled down. Shortly after, a still more serious, even a grave, incident took place, an incident that had to do with the person of Francis Joseph.

On 15 January 1857 the Emperor, who was touring through his Empire with much pomp and circumstance, made a solemn entry into Milan. It was the day chosen by the head of the Piedmontese Government for launching in Parliament these winged words: "You will remember that in Byron's time, lovers of Italy looked upon her as a beautiful woman in the power of a barbarous and tyrannical spouse. They pitied her, of course, but they believed her dedicated to eternal oppression because they believed her incapable of ruling herself. That time is no more. Conscious of her power, and of the sympathy she has found abroad, Italy is now striding towards independence and liberty! . . ." The Official Gazette did not fail to emphasise the boldness of this speech; it announced, too, that the municipality of Turin was about to accept a subscription offered by the Milanese to raise a monument on the banks of the Po to the Piedmontese army, the army that had so gallantly carried the Italian flag before Sevastopol. The Ballplatz thought this was going too far. After a rapid exchange of peevish notes, Count Paar was recalled to Vienna.

Neither the French nor British Government approved of the brusque attitude of the Piedmontese Government in a quarrel that might prove dangerous to the peace of Europe, and they did not hesitate to show their disapproval. Cavour detected a profound difference between the remonstrances that emanated from the two capitals. The language held by Sir James Hudson in Lord Palmerston's name unquestionably expressed the decided and deliberate opinion of the British Government, regardless of what the consequences might be. But in what measure did the remonstrances formulated by the Duc de Gramont in the name of Comte Walewski express the secret convictions of Napoleon III, who, after all, was the master in France? What precisely were the secret convictions of the Sphinx of the Tuileries? Where had his hidden dreams led him? That was the vexed problem confronting Cavour, a problem into the solving of which he threw all his gifts of intellect and of penetration.

The personal letters Cavour addressed to the Marquis Villamarina, Piedmontese Minister at Paris, reveal his perplexity, show what he knew and what he did not know, what he hoped and what he feared. On 18 February he wrote: "Count Paar's note is conceived in a tone that indicates that the Austrian Cabinet is determined to intimidate us. I can assure you that it will not succeed in doing so. We are not in the least disposed to yield to threats even were we certain these would be followed up by action. . . . *I have too great confidence in the lofty aims of the Emperor Napoleon, and in his friendship for us, to believe for a moment that he would counsel us to show any weakness*; that would be suicide; but I believe that Walewski allows only instructions more or less favourable to the pretensions of Austria to be given to Gramont. . . ." On 21 February Cavour wrote again: "However much I might wish to second the views of France, I shall not advise the King to the least act of weakness towards Austria. If the Cabinet at Vienna carries out its threats and withdraws its legation from Turin, we shall have no objection to offer provided France does not countenance the step. If it goes further and threatens recourse to arms, we shall not take the offensive; but we shall be ready to give them a good reception. The best spirit rules in the army and in the country. I am certain that our soldiers, led by the King and La Marmora, will repulse an army three times as large as ours. Neither I nor anyone else can foretell what is going to happen. But I think we are still far from so extreme a contingency, and I think that Austria will hesitate long before firing the cannon that will awaken in Europe *the great cause of nationalities.*" On 19 March Cavour wrote to one of his colleagues, Count Oldofredi, who was in Paris : " When opportunity offers to speak of us, tell everyone that we are prudent, that we are quite calmly awaiting eventualities, but that if we are called upon to act we shall show ourselves determined to risk everything for the honour and the safety of our country. *If it comes to the point, we shall show ourselves refractory children.*"

V

While Europe was assembled in Congress in Paris, Cavour had taken care to secure for himself as many sources of information and influence as possible for future use. He left behind him in Paris many faithful interpreters of his ideals, many sincere friends of the Italian cause ; for the most part these were people of lesser social consequence who yet had the invaluable privilege, in Cavour's eyes, of access to the Emperor through devious and secret ways gratifying to his conspiratorial instincts. Of all these the most valuable was Dr. Conneau. Born in Milan in 1803, the son of a French father and a Lombard mother, physician to the Bonaparte family during their residence in Rome about 1830, he regarded Prince Louis Napoleon with friendship and affection, and had wholeheartedly devoted himself to his service. For six years he had shared Napoleon's captivity

9

in Ham. Now "Physician-in-chief to the Emperor," and honoured with his entire confidence, he approached him whenever he wished. With this man Cavour did not directly correspond; their accustomed intermediary was the former fighter in the Romagna, the former exile in New York, Count Arese, who had become a Senator in the Piedmontese Parliament.

After Conneau, Madame Hortense Cornu was the most zealous advocate of Cavour's ideas. A strange woman: plain, disdaining all finery, an idealist and free-thinker, high-minded and strong-willed, a disinterested intriguer, she had passed her entire youth with Queen Hortense, to whom her mother, Madame Lacroix, was waiting-woman. A real or supposititious motherhood? Singular rumours were current. It was alleged that the waiting-woman had rendered her mistress a service which had not been less necessary in the case of Morny. However that may be, the young girl, brought up side by side with Louis Napoleon and the comrade of his youth, soon became more than a companion, more even than a friend—became indeed a sister, watching over him, zealous in his service, brave, stimulating, admiring, but stiff, puritanical, distrustful, and tyrannical. Grateful for her passionate devotion, Louis Napoleon made her the repository of all his dreams and projects. Married in 1834 to an undistinguished painter, Sebastian Cornu, who painted very indifferent scenes for the museum at Versailles, she led a life of restraint and respectability. Finding little satisfaction in the daily round, impelled by an insatiable desire to find employment for her active mind, she devoted herself to a noble cause: the enfranchisement and regeneration of the nations. She was in communication with the leading revolutionaries of Italy, Poland, Spain, Hungary, Germany, and Russia—with all the chief plotters in Europe. In 1837, on his return from America, Louis Napoleon confided to her and Conneau alone the solemn engagements into which he had entered in New York. While he was a prisoner at Ham she was lavish in her demonstrations of affection and in her endeavours to console him. In 1848 his elevation to the Presidency of the Republic filled her with joy; but the Second of December destroyed her love for him. She looked upon him as a perjurer, and refused to see him again. In vain Napoleon III endeavoured to soften her, and to induce her to accept an allowance that would at least have tempered the rigours of her poverty. Only after the birth of the Prince Imperial did she consent to resume their friendship. Her visits to the Tuileries were few and far between, and when she came she entered by a private way. The Empress hated her, fearing her influence with the Emperor, and knowing very well the subject of their cabals. Fortune greatly favoured Cavour in sending him such an agent.

After Dr. Conneau and Madame Cornu, Cavour's most useful agent was a fellow-countryman, though a naturalised Frenchman, Alexander Bixio. Ardent republican and noted agriculturist, he had taken part in the Constituent Assembly of 1848, and Lamartine, whose *chef de cabinet* he was, had sent him on a special mission to Turin. Through Bixio Cavour entered into permanent relations with the small liberal and censorious circle of the Palais-Royal. Although Prince Napoleon had already been converted to the Italian cause, the important part he was to play in the *Risorgimento* did not begin until the decisive hour came at the close of 1858.

The Machiavellian cleverness of Cavour suggested a device by which he would be assured of an even more intimate way of approach to Napoleon III. He laid in the Imperial bed a superb creature of twenty-one, beautiful and daring as a patrician of the Renaissance, decorative and sumptuous as one of Titian's courtesans : Countess Castiglione. Descended from an ancient Tuscan house, the Oldoïni, related to Cavour, her birth was veiled in mystery ; she herself declared that she was a daughter of a Polish prince, scion of a royal house. Her husband, a very brave man, was passionately devoted to her, but she refused to have anything to do with him and he suffered and pined in silence. While perfecting his plan for the Congress of Paris, Cavour took notice of her and, in his own words, " enrolled her in the diplomatic service of Italy " with the order " to flirt with the Emperor." She thoroughly understood what was required of her, being no less ambitious than she was magnificent, and Cavour had no need to say by way of encouragement : " Succeed, my cousin, by whatever means you please ; but succeed ! " The beautiful Florentine made her bow to Parisian society at a reception given by Princesse Mathilde to which she had been invited at the express desire of the Marquis Villamarina. She was a brilliant success ! Every man was at her feet : every woman filled with fury. The chief chamberlain, Bacciochi, a faithful servant, gave an exact account of her appearance to his master ; and the affair progressed as had been intended. The modern Judith piously immolated herself in the service of her country.

Not that her sacrifice would seem to have left too painful
memories behind, if one can judge from that laſt clause of
her will written forty years later : "I desire to be buried
in my cambric and lace nightgown that I wore at Compiègne."
The Emperor quickly wearied of her, for, despite her Olym-
pian beauty, she lacked naturalness, charm, and liveliness.
Their liaison laſted, with several interruptions, only two
years. But during those two years—years of capital importance in Cavour's lifework—the voluptuous Florentine
was well employed in creating what Properce called " romantic
occasions for conversation." *Mollia fandi tempora.*

VI

Throughout the spring of 1857 Napoleon III was more
enigmatic and baffling than ever. The Congress of Paris
had scarcely brought its deliberations to a close than perilous
visions dazzled his eyes. Before he yielded to their seduĉtions,
however, fear seemed to lay its quickening finger upon him,
and a mood of caution supervened.

On 16 May 1856 he welcomed to Saint-Cloud the future
martyr of Querataro, the Archduke Maximilian of Auſtria.
That evening he took Baron Hübner aside and conversed
with him for nearly an hour. Immediately broaching the
Italian Queſtion, he said : " I have entered into an alliance
with England, and, on the other hand, the co-operation
of the Piedmontese army in the Crimea entitles King Viĉtor
Emmanuel to my sympathy. *But I am afraid leſt the current
sweeps me away ; I am terribly afraid. . . .*" Hübner replied
that if France allied herself with the policy of England and
Piedmont she would be loſt for ever in the whirlpool of

revolutionary forces. He added: " You will bring upon Europe as much evil as you have already brought good, and you will do no one more harm than yourself." " True," replied the Emperor; " and that is why I am so uneasy." Hübner then asked him a direct question: " Have you any intention, Sire, of bringing about territorial changes in Italy?" " None whatever," answered Napoleon. " In that case," continued Hübner, " why do we not come to an understanding between ourselves?" " That is exactly what I ask myself," said the Emperor. " We so nearly understand one another, Austria and I!"

But the fascination of the Italian adventure quickly gained the upper hand in Napoleon's tortured mind. On 27 May, seven days after his conversation with Hübner at Saint-Cloud, when Marshal Vaillant, Minister for War, came to make his customary report to him at the Tuileries, the Emperor said brusquely: " I wish to have ready an army to enter Italy. Find out how the Army of the Alps was constituted in 1848, and whether it is possible to place the nucleus of an army on the Savoyard frontier." Next day the Marshal brought him an historical account of the measures taken in 1848, in addition to a plan for making the garrison of Lyons into a concentration centre with a strength of 26,000 men. Approving the plan, Napoleon gave orders for it to be published throughout the army. " I desire," he said, " to have five corps always ready for active service." The Marshal bowed; only very gradually did he come to understand what was passing in the Imperial mind, for soon afterwards he declared with surprise that his Sovereign had not mentioned the matter to him again.

From that day the growth of an obsession can be observed in Napoleon's mind—an obsession irritated by the bitterness inspired in him when prevented from commanding his armies at Sevastopol. According to the testimony of Madame Cornu, " he had dreamed since infancy of a war that should chase the Austrians out of Italy and in which he would hold the command." Once during his imprisonment at Ham he said to her : " I know I shall one day command a great army ; I know I shall cover myself with glory ; I know I possess great military ability." He had made his decision. In the approaching war—inevitable since Austria would never give up her Italian provinces unless compelled to do so by force of arms—he himself would hold the supreme command. Nor did his want of experience and ignorance of strategy deter him one whit. His whole military training consisted of the technical knowledge of gunnery acquired in the artillery school at Thun. He had never commanded a brigade or even a regiment. Nevertheless, he should be generalissimo ; only then would he feel the full consciousness of his divine mission : *Cæsar Imperator*.

In order to learn that art of war of which Gustavus, Turenne, and Frederick II were masters, and in which his own great ancestor—the demi-god of war—outshone all others, Napoleon caused a huge camp, extending over more than twenty-five thousand acres, to be set up in the plain of Champagne at Chalons. He never tired of superintending the preparation of the ground, the building of roads, of forts, and of barracks. On 29 August 1857 he had the triumph of seeing the Imperial Guard, three regiments of Grenadiers four regiments of infantry, a regiment of Zouaves, a battalion of light infantry, two regiments of Cuirassiers, a regiment of Dragoons and one of Lancers, a regiment of Guides and two regiments of Artillery, in all 22,000 men and 5,000 horses, manœuvre under his command.

Relations between Paris and Vienna were meanwhile becoming strained and embittered. Misunderstandings, disputes, wranglings, mutual recriminations, continued as before, and the French Minister for Foreign Affairs, the wise and courageous Walewski, though sensing the gravity of the situation, could do nothing to oppose the secret and underhand intrigues of his master. Hübner also beheld what the future had in store. On 8 February 1857 he wrote to Count Buol : " The Emperor, whom I had the honour to meet at a Court ball, is reserved, and avoids discussing politics with me. We must be on our guard lest we receive a *coup de Jarnac*." On 13 May he wrote in words that reveal his fine judgment : " One day in 1849 or 1850, when Napoleon was, so to say, a prisoner of State at the Élysée, he said to me : ' *Louis Philippe has been overthrown because he permitted France to fall into disrepute. I must do something !* ' That belief led him into the Crimea. Since then his years have increased, and weigh heavily upon him. He is bordering upon fifty. At this age with good health already put to the test, with a charming wife and a child upon whom all his father's hopes centre, with the means to gratify every desire, with a brilliant position extraordinarily attained, *truly he would be a fool to risk all this without rhyme or reason*." Similar language was held to Napoleon III by all his counsellors, ministers, and ambassadors whenever he deigned to open his mind to them.

From whatever angle it was surveyed, the idea of the Italian adventure appeared so completely divorced from reality, so unreasonable, and so utterly opposed to the ancient political traditions of France, that even Mazzini himself refused to believe that the former conspirator of the Romagna intended to keep his word. "No one in reason could believe that Louis Napoleon would wish to create by the unification of Italy a Power that could rival France; that he would wish, by means of a long war and the consequent dissolution of Austria, to leave the field open to the revolutionary principle of nationality."

The dreamer in the Tuileries seems to have become sensible, towards the end of September, of the general disquiet aroused among even the most fervent believers in the Napoleonic creed, by the new and now public orientation of his foreign policy. Throughout his career he was always sensitive to public opinion, and, though he was rarely guided by it, he sought to dupe when he could not satisfy it. At the zenith of his career this was the easier for him in that his dissimulation was still mistaken for profundity; his desperate throws for deliberate audacity; his wonted indecision for far-sightedness. Two incidents occurred to deepen this impression.

On 28 September he met the Emperor Alexander II at Stuttgart. Great hopes were laid by Napoleon not only on Russia's keeping the German States in check and protecting his Rhine frontier while he fought against Austria in the valley of the Po, but also when he was engaged in reducing the terrible quadrilateral of Verona. The presence of the French and Russian Ministers for Foreign Affairs, Count Walewski and Prince Gortchakoff, revealed the importance of the interview. But the Tsar, under a cloak of great courtesy, displayed so great a reserve towards Napoleon that their conversation was of a purely academic nature. Except for a passing allusion, not a word was said about Italy. A vague promise " to concert in future on all European questions " was given and received, but it was not even consigned to a protocol. Farewells were exchanged, and Alexander II departed for Weimar to meet—Francis Joseph !

Meanwhile, matters had been going badly in Piedmont, where Cavour was involved in serious political difficulties. The mandate of the Chamber having expired, a general election ensued. Under active intimidation from the clerical and reactionary parties, the electors returned a Chamber hostile to those liberal principles on which rested the whole adventure of the *Risorgimento*. Finding itself with an infinitesimal majority, the Government resigned. Although the shock of defeat had been great and unexpected, Cavour never faltered. Determined not to permit the future of Italy to be destroyed by " a jesuitical conspiracy hatched in the sacristies throughout the kingdom," he threw down the gauntlet to his opponents and managed matters so well that in a fresh election he emerged with a restored majority. The alarm had been great, and it took time for the Piedmontese Machiavelli to recover his reputation both at home and abroad. The year 1857 thus ended unpropitiously for the Italian cause. No star of hope arose in the months that followed.

It would not be surprising, moreover, if the natural tendencies of Napoleon III led him to that state of mind in which he often revelled : a state of shuffling, of hazy uncertainty, of soporific contemplation of far horizons, of confused meditation upon the rôle conferred on him by Providence and his ancestry. . . . What an awakening was at hand !

At half-past eight on the evening of 14 January 1858, as the Emperor and Empress arrived at the Opera (then standing in the Rue Le Peletier), three terrific explosions like three claps of thunder, and practically simultaneous, killed the horses of the Imperial carriage, shattered the glass doors, and extinguished the illuminations on the front of the Opera-house and all the street-lamps. The sudden darkness was filled with cries of fear and pain. The victims numbered one hundred and fifty-seven : lancers of the escort, municipal guards, policemen, footmen, innocent onlookers, among whom were twenty women and a dozen children.

Amidst the general panic the Emperor and Empress, saved as by a miracle, stepped calmly from their wrecked carriage. With blanched faces and horror-stricken eyes, they entered the Imperial box to rounds of applause. The performance took place as though nothing had happened. Before the night was over, accident delivered up to the police the authors of the outrage : four Italians. A Tuscan, Piéri ; a Venetian, Rudio ; a Neapolitan, Gomez ; and the leader, Orsini, from the Romagna. It seemed as though all the provinces of the Peninsula had sought to participate in the assassination. A swift trial of the prisoners followed. On 25 February the accused were brought before the Court. The trial did not last long, for there was no doubt about the crime or the identity of the criminals. From the outset it was realised Piéri, Rudio, and Gomez were merely accomplices. Orsini held the stage.

With his first words a wave of sympathy surged over the Court. A curious psychological phenomenon of collective suggestion transformed Orsini from an assassin into a hero. This may have been due in part to his striking and virile appearance. Tall and broad-shouldered, with a high forehead, aquiline nose, and superb eyes, a voice both solemn and pleading, a reticence in the use of gesture, well dressed, he spoke in a measured, cultivated, and distinguished manner. Disdaining his trembling accomplices, he took upon himself the entire responsibility for the tragedy: without boasting or arrogance, with the quiet detachment of a man who had long ago dedicated his life. Every eye was upon him, every ear listened to him in an admiring and fascinated silence. So great was his personal magnetism that it penetrated beyond the walls of the Court into the streets, the fashionable world, even into the Tuileries. The Austrian ambassador, Hübner, notes in his diary that " the Empress herself is infatuated with the handsome assassin."

Orsini seemed even more of a hero to the audience that filled the Court on the following, and what promised to be the last, day of the trial. The speech of the counsel for the defence, Jules Favre, contributed not a little to produce this effect. Fully conscious of all the interests at stake in the trial, feeling that the hopes of a nation depended upon him, realising that he was in truth speaking before the tribunal of History, stimulated by the atmosphere in which he spoke, the great advocate soared to the supreme heights of his eloquence.

Employing a style at once classical, rhythmical, and subtle, he recalled to his hearers the antecedents of the accused, whose father, a former officer of the Napoleonic armies, "had mingled his blood with ours on many battle-fields." He depicted this aged survivor of Wagram and Moscow as participating in the insurrection in the Romagna in 1831, "attacking the Papal throne in company *with illustrious accomplices*," and finally sharing in the rout at Spoleto. "Felix Orsini," Favre continued, "was twelve years of age when he beheld these misfortunes. He saw his home broken up, his father a fugitive, exiled, condemned to a wanderer's life. Is it surprising that fiery and relentless hatred arose in his boyish heart to inspire him against the enemies of his country?" The defence seemed to be concluded with these words. But there came a sudden, dramatic turn. Before the impassive judges and the stupefied audience Jules Favre read out a letter addressed to the Emperor by the accused as his last will and testament: "The depositions I have made suffice to send me to my death, to which I will submit without asking pardon: I will not humble myself before the destroyer of the nascent freedom of my unhappy fatherland. I only wish to make one final effort on behalf of Italy. I summon Your Majesty to give her that independence which the French lost to her in 1849. . . . Remember, Your Majesty, that unless Italy is free, the peace of Your Majesty and of the rest of Europe will be no more than an illusion! Your Majesty will not spurn the last wish of a patriot standing on the very steps of the scaffold. Deliver my fatherland and the blessing of twenty-five million of its citizens will be upon you for ever!" To this sad appeal, Jules Favre added a sentence which concluded his plea on a note of religious lyricism, with the amplitude and grave dignity of a funeral oration. " I have no more to say, gentlemen. You will do your duty without passion and without weakness. But God, Who judges us all ; God, before Whom all the great of this world, deprived of their attendant courtiers and flatterers, appear in their naked verity ; God, Who alone judges our sins and the expiation that effaces them ; God will pronounce His judgment after yours, and He will not refuse to pardon him to whom pardon was refused upon earth ! "

Despite Favre's brilliant speech, the verdict was as inscribed beforehand in the registrar's records. For Orsini, Rudio, and Piéri, the death penalty ; for Gomez, the galleys for life. The Emperor, under pressure from the Empress, desired to pardon the three condemned men. But his ministers and the Cabinet represented to him with great force that to safeguard his dynasty from further attempts of a like nature a merciless repression must be maintained, and the law permitted to take its course. On 13 March, at dawn, the guillotine was set up on the Place de la Roquette. To the last Orsini maintained his proud intrepidity. Before the knife fell he cried in a courageous voice : " Long live Italy ! "

Throughout the entire course of this great judicial drama nothing had so amazed contemporary opinion as Orsini's letter to the Emperor, and above all, the fact that the presiding judge had permitted it to be read aloud. Even to-day the episode presents a difficult problem to historians. Was Orsini really the writer of the letter ? If the question be answered in the affirmative, how came he to write it ? a letter

apparently disavowing his deed of 14 January, and leaving
the fate of Italy in the hands of the man he had sought to
kill. No doubt longer exists concerning the authorship of
the letter. It did not emanate directly from Orsini ; it was
drafted by Jules Favre. If read carefully, it reveals the
style and oratorical traits of the great advocate. It might
have formed part of a counsel's pleading. When he had
agreed to, and doubtless a little accentuated, the draft, Orsini
translated it into Italian and signed it. By accepting it, he
appropriated to himself the words and the ideas. But even
Jules Favre was not the true author of the letter. He only
drafted it on an inspiration emanating from a very exalted
source, from the Emperor himself, through the intermediary
of the Prefect of Police, Pietri. This official—a senator
and Napoleon's principal agent in his secret undertakings
—came to confer with Orsini in his prison cell and sought
to convince him of " the great misguidedness of his deed,
the folly of having sought to kill the only powerful and
disinterested friend of the Italian cause in Europe." So
impassioned were the words of the Imperial envoy, so
pressing were his arguments, that the would-be assassin felt
" as though a bandage had been torn from his eyes." The
utter foolishness of his crime became apparent to him, and
he understood for the first time that Napoleon III, instead of
being an obstacle in the way of the enfranchisement of Italy,
was the sole person capable of carrying it through. Suddenly
perceiving new hopes rising above the horizon, he consented to sign the letter. Nevertheless, in a final outburst
of pride, he insisted that it should be made clear that in
addressing his last appeal to the Emperor he did not ask

a pardon for himself, "for he would never humiliate himself before the destroyer of the nascent freedom of his fatherland."

The mission of the Prefect of Police to the accused requires a word of explanation. A mission all the more significant in that it was contrary to all the rules of criminal procedure, and which the President of the Court would never have tolerated unless expressly ordered to do so. Why did the Emperor inspire this appeal to his own person on behalf of the Italian people? The first thought that occurs to the mind is that Orsini's attempt had terrified Napoleon III— an explanation to which the Prince Consort has given the weight of his authority; while the war of 1859 was later ascribed by the Emperor Francis Joseph, Pius IX, and the old Prince Metternich, to Napoleon's fear of assassination. Pure calumny! Throughout the whole course of his life Napoleon III gave too many proofs of his courage for its existence to be doubted. He was by nature brave with a simple bravery that never varied, and in which nobility of soul and a chivalrous spirit played at least as great a part as his fatalistic resignation. But if, on the evening of 14 January, Napoleon certainly did not display the humiliating agony of physical fear, can it be affirmed that he did not entertain the liveliest fears for his throne and his dynasty? While the private individual remained impassive, the head of the State, the restorer of the Empire, the autocratic Cæsar who believed that he and he alone could assure the greatness and prosperity of France—this man had the right to be afraid.

By the illuminating flash of their explosion, the bombs

hurled by Orsini and his accomplices revealed to Napoleon III the execration in which he was held by the Italian revolutionaries. When with an "impious cynicism" he had overthrown the Roman Republic in order to seat himself on the throne of France, Mazzini had written to him : "You have broken your sacred vows : you have betrayed the God of your youth!" Since that day the followers of Mazzini had been possessed by the idea of assassinating him ; for them it had become the dominating thought, the primordial aim, "a deed imperatively necessary, almost a religious act, which was indispensable to the salvation of the people." Each bore the sentence of death engraved upon his heart. To this fact the foiled plots of Pianori in 1855 and Tibaldi in 1857 bore witness.

Even in the first radiant years of the Empire, amidst the glittering splendours of the young Court, in the fêtes continually given at the Tuileries, Fontainebleau, and Compiègne, there can often be discerned in the Emperor a fear of the future ; the feeling that his throne is precarious ; that the imperial edifice would crumble at a touch. Often there can be divined in the innermost recesses of his mind the unwelcome vision of his Italian past :

> "Quoniam medio de fonte leporum
> Surgit amari aliquid, quod in ipsis floribus angat ;
> Aut quum conscius ipse animus se forte remordet."

How then could he avoid seeing the terrible menace inspiring Orsini's phrase : "Unless Italy is free, the peace of Your Majesty and of the rest of Europe will be no more than an illusion" ? How fail to comprehend that for him

10

the enfranchisement of Italy had become a vital necessity, and that if he desired to safeguard his throne he must by an irrevocable gesture give hope to Italian patriots?

For this reason he secured from Orsini on the eve of his execution a second letter more explicit than the first : " The sympathy of Your Majesty for Italy is no small comfort to me in my last moments. Before I draw my last breath, I declare that assassination, no matter under what pretext, is not to be found among my principles, although by a fatal aberration I organised the attempt on 14 January. Let my fellow-countrymen learn from my lips that instead of trusting to assassination they will assure the deliverance of Italy by their self-sacrifice, devotion, and union alone."

In order to give these two letters their fullest significance and import the Emperor needed the help of Cavour.

CHAPTER V

THE INTERVIEW AT PLOMBIÈRES

CHAPTER V

THE INTERVIEW AT PLOMBIÈRES

I

THE news of the attempted assassination reached Turin on 15 January 1858. "Let us hope they are not Italians," said Cavour. An hour later a telegram containing the names of the would-be murderers arrived: Orsini, Rudio, Piéri, Gomez—all Italians! Orsini's name aroused a faint recollection in Cavour. Some months previously he had received a letter from Orsini in which he offered to provoke an insurrection in Rome. Fortunately, Cavour had been sensible enough to leave the letter unanswered. Cavour was overwhelmed by this event. Was all his work about to go for nothing? Eight years of labour! Were all the hopes of Italy to be destroyed by the impetuous folly of a fanatic? For, indeed, without the French alliance, there could be no *Risorgimento*. But this alliance depended solely upon Napoleon, the master of France; and how could his interest and sympathy in the liberation of a nation be retained when it kept sending assassins to kill him? As the news of the fury which possessed the Parisian populace, and their outcries against Italy, reached him during the succeeding days, Cavour's anxiety increased. Panic reigned in Paris, where it seemed to excited imaginations that the Napoleonic edifice was already levelled to the ground and revolution master in its place. Even the Emperor lost his head. At a parliamentary reception on the second day after the attempt the crowd were startled by his pallor and depression. His behaviour revealed what effect the nervous strain had had upon his mind. In swift succession he published formidable edicts to safeguard public order ; a general became Minister for the Interior ; France was divided up into five great military districts, each commanded by a marshal ; the penal code was strengthened : a Bill was laid before the Chamber giving to the administrative authorities powers of expulsion, internment, and exile of all suspected persons. These measures were the more arbitrary and unreasonable because in fact no Frenchman had been concerned in the attempted assassination on 14 January, which had been conceived and organised abroad by foreigners in order to promote the objects of a foreign cause. At the same time, Walewski addressed notes, couched in a tone of considerable irritation, to the neighbouring governments—England, Belgium, Switzerland, and Piedmont—demanding that they should take severe measures both against the assassins who had taken refuge within their frontiers and against the newspapers in whose columns they had found the inspiration for their deed and who had subsequently sung their praises. In London these demands, emphasised by foolish demonstrations in the French army, aroused a hurricane of indignation, and Palmerston—that doughty champion of British arrogance—was forced to resign the Premiership because he had not given a strong enough reply to the French ambassador.

Between Turin and Paris a no less violent conflict arose. Walewski ordered Prince de La Tour d'Auvergne, who had replaced the Duc de Gramont as minister on the latter's promotion to the ambassadorship at Rome, to read to Cavour a harsh despatch in which Piedmont was arraigned as the protector of the enemies of European society in general, and which concluded with a demand for the expulsion of the revolutionary refugees, the restriction of the liberty of the press, and the interdiction of any contributions sent by refugees to the newspapers. To these imperative demands Cavour replied with the exclamation, " You are asking me to effect a *coup d'état* ! " When La Tour d'Auvergne insisted on their fulfilment, Cavour's pride was aroused. " Charles Albert," he said, " died in Portugal rather than bow the knee to Austria. Our youthful King would sooner die at the foot of the Alps than see his escutcheon spotted. While as for us, his ministers, we will follow him. We are sworn foes to revolution. We hate assassins as much as you do ; but we are also Liberals, because we believe that liberty alone can save Italy. And Liberals we will remain, even though in doing so we forfeit your valued friendship. At the very least we will fall flag in hand and with our honour unstained." But Cavour was not the man to allow himself to be caught in an impasse, still less was he the man to place himself in one. The problem was at one and the same time to prevent any insult to the dignity of Piedmont while preserving the indispensable friendship of France. His keen appreciation of the situation suggested a solution to him, and, continuing to refuse the arbitrary demands made upon him, he consented to bring forward the draft of a law by which, without in any way interfering with the fundamental liberties of the kingdom, the persons of foreign sovereigns might be more effectively guarded against the attacks of revolutionaries.

Throughout this acrimonious controversy with the French Government the King gave him undeviating support. In order to soothe Napoleon's anger Victor Emmanuel dispatched his personal aide-de-camp General Della Rocca to Paris with an autograph letter. At first Della Rocca was coldly received by the Emperor. Customarily calm and suave, Napoleon on this occasion showed himself no less harsh and surly than Walewski had been. When speaking of the demonstrations of loyalty provoked in his regiments by the attempt on his life, he even went so far as to declare that: "My army is determined to rout out any den of assassins, no matter where it may lie." When this insult was reported to Victor Emmanuel he leapt as though all the blood of his ancestors had rushed to his heart; and he wrote to Della Rocca: "If the words which you have reported to me are the exact words used by the Emperor, tell him that he does not treat me as a faithful ally should be treated; that I have never endured an insult from anyone; that I walk in the path of honour and duty, and that for this honour and duty I am responsible solely to God and my people; that for eight hundred years we have held our heads high and no one has been able to cast us down; finally, that I have no other desire except to be his friend." And he added: "You will be so *imprudent* as to read this letter to the Emperor." Della Rocca's imprudence was in the highest degree successful. Napoleon III was too chivalrous not to sense the bravery and splendid kingliness which inspired this letter. Nor could he be insensible to those eight hundred years of unbroken rule which made the House of Savoy the doyen of all the reigning houses of Europe—he whose renown was so recent, who had not even been born to the throne, and who had avowed himself to be " a parvenu among the old monarchs." Both the style and tone of the letter moved him so deeply that he exclaimed : " Behold what it is to have courage ! Your king is a brave man. I admire his letter. Write to him immediately, and allay his doubts of me." A few days later when, on the eve of his departure from Paris, Della Rocca was received in audience, the Emperor told him that should Austria attack Piedmont, a French army would come to Piedmont's help. He concluded by saying : " Tell M. Cavour that he should write to me and that we are certain to understand one another."

The King's letter was not the sole cause of this great result. Cavour's faithful helpers, Dr. Conneau, Alexander Bixio, the severe Madame Cornu, the gallant and voluptuous Countess de Castiglione, all contributed to it. The situation was rapidly, though in secret, transformed. Walewski, however, continued to remain in ignorance of what was passing, and to launch against Piedmont his harmless thunderbolts. All doubts were resolved, and Fortune once more smiled upon Cavour.

Fortune was even kinder than he imagined. On 13 March—the day on which the head of Orsini fell severed by the guillotine's stroke—by Napoleon's orders the Piedmontese minister in Paris was handed the correspondence of the executed criminal with authority to publish it in the Official Gazette of Turin. If Cavour was audacious, he was not foolhardy. From the beginning he felt no little apprehension at the idea of transfiguring the memory of a regicide in a kind of apotheosis. What an example, what an encouragement for Mazzini! And what was to be said to Austria? Would she not regard it as an intolerable insult? Hence he ordered Villamarina to make his objections known at the Tuileries. Nevertheless, the answer came, "Publish." Cavour no longer desisted. On 31 March the official journal of Piedmont published the political testament of the martyr. In Italy, and throughout Europe, the effect produced was tremendous; it was more than a dramatic stroke; it was a clap of thunder.

II

Cavour had now penetrated to the innermost thoughts of Napoleon III. This spring of 1858 found Napoleon in a psychological state that revealed the deepest traits in his vacillating personality. Predominant among these was an imaginative exaltation of spirit, a tendency to indulge in day-dreams, and in fanciful and confused speculations. Like all dreamers, he never wearied of making plans, elaborating theories, and building up systems. Lord Palmerston said of him: "The head of Napoleon III is a veritable rabbit-warren out of which ideas are continually coming forth like rabbits." Yet this man who had achieved so much in his life was essentially not a man of action. He was incapable of seeing the wood for the trees; incapable of immediate, clear, and concrete perception. The dazzling visions glowing in the far reaches of his soul lured his eye from what lay directly in his path. He was like a traveller with eyes fixed upon a distant view who sees little of the country through

NAPOLEON III.

which he passes, or of the natural obstacles, rivers, mountains, marches, precipices, and chasms that bar his road. Thus it came about that his calculations were never justified in the result; that his schemes never worked out according to plan. And, as he was always at issue with men and affairs, seemed vacillating, out of his element, confusedly calculating the many chances and alternatives, adopting a sphinx-like stare and surrounding himself with an atmosphere of mystery in order to conceal his doubts and indecisions, at times falling into a torpor of discouragement, a bleak and lethargic fatalism, then, rousing himself suddenly because his star was again in the ascendant, he provoked a crisis by an impulsive, theatrical, and resounding gesture.

Unhappily for himself and for France, he believed that he was destined to accomplish great things. Three motives actuated him in this belief. First, his belief in the destiny of his family and in the mission which Providence had conferred upon the Bonapartes. With him this belief amounted to an inner faith, as unquestionable and authoritative as a religious dogma. In his *Histoire de César* he peremptorily affirms the divine right of heroes: " When Providence raises up men like Cæsar, Charlemagne, and Napoleon, it does so in order to point out to the nations the way in which they should walk. Happy are the peoples who understand and follow these leaders! Cursed are those who do not recognise them and who fight against them!" He was hypnotised by the glorious traditions of the First Empire: to renew those glories was his consuming ambition. One might almost say he feared lest his uncle should arise from his grave to curse him unless he sought the inspiration for his deeds in that sublime epic. Moreover, that redoubtable uncle who slept in the Invalides had in some measure allotted to him his task, when he declared at St. Helena in prophetic words : " The first monarch who in the midst of general unrest truly embraces the cause of the people will win for himself the hegemony of Europe and will be able to do whatever he desires."

For Napoleon III the enfranchisement of the nations meant more than a mere humanitarian and philosophical idea ; it became matter for political calculation. Through emancipating oppressed peoples he would restore France to her former greatness. Yet another, and less elevated, motive inspired him. In his opinion, the fall of the July Monarchy was mainly due to its prosaicness, bourgeois character, and weak foreign policy. Hence he resolved never to fall into Louis Philippe's error, but on every opportunity to increase the prestige of France. Then, having deprived the French of their civil liberties, simple prudence would require that he should turn their attention away from home affairs and excite their imagination at the same time as he flattered their national spirit by affording them the unceasing spectacle of a France brilliant and powerful above all other nations. Thus he visualised a rôle as sovereign for which he had neither the temperament nor the abilities. Simultaneously he should be the liberator of the peoples and the pacificator of the world. He conceived of himself as a supreme arbiter, a *deus ex machina*, into whose hands had been entrusted the high duty of apportioning kingdoms and lands ; of composing great international disputes and secular antagonisms between the races.

A man who knew him well and who, above all others, was capable of understanding him, for their spirits had much in common, Émile Ollivier, said of him: "Napoleon III desires as far as possible to upset the world in order that, as a consequence, he may be called upon to act as a judge before a sort of œcumenical council which in its importance and the novelty of its decisions will efface the Congress of Vienna." But another man, with much practical experience of him, for on four occasions he had been his Minister for Foreign Affairs, Drouyn de Lhuys, said with greater truth: "The Emperor is endowed with immense desires and limited capacities. He seeks to achieve extraordinary things and he accomplishes only extravagant ones."

III

When the Orsini correspondence was published in the Official Gazette at Turin the European chancelleries at once suspected the conclusion of a secret treaty between France and Piedmont. The Prince Consort, in whom Napoleon III inspired instinctive distrust, and who was always on the watch for plottings in the Tuileries, at once perceived what lay behind the publication. On 20 April he wrote to his old friend Baron Stockmar: "I fear that the Emperor contemplates a dramatic stroke in Italy which would serve him as a lightning-conductor. Since Orsini's attempt, he has strongly favoured the cause of Italian independence. But the Pope and the Concordat stand in his way. A conflict between Piedmont and Naples, in which he would not openly participate, would set Italy ablaze. All is ready for

the burning, and so abundant is the fuel that it would suffice
to light a fire that might reach even to Germany."

It would seem to have been in April 1858 that Napoleon
III resolved to make war upon Austria. Thenceforth he
spent long hours in his study, poring over maps of Northern
Italy, and studying the course of the Po, the by-roads of
the Tessin and the Adda, the undulating plain of the Mincio,
the passes of the Adige—in short, all the immense Cisalpine
district where the immortal names of Montenotte, Castiglione,
Arcola, Rivoli, and Marengo stand forth like brilliant stars
in the night. Early in May he gave audience to General
MacMahon, whom he esteemed for his very real ability,
although his legitimist leanings caused him to be regarded
with suspicion in the Tuileries. Swearing him to secrecy,
Napoleon laid bare to him the scheme he had been revolving
in his mind, and, in conclusion, ordered him to go as a simple
tourist to investigate the fortifications at Milan, Brescia,
Verona, Mantua, Venice, and Pola. Equally preoccupied
with calculations as to the military support which Piedmont
would be able to afford him, the Emperor never received
the Marquis Villamarina without questioning him about the
strength of the fortifications at Casal and Alessandria. So
marked did the Emperor's importunity become that the
Piedmontese minister wrote to Cavour : " Taking everything
into consideration, I believe that the Emperor means to
wage war." At the same moment, and as if to confirm
Villamarina's opinion, Alexander Bixio—that familiar spirit
of the Palais-Royal—forwarded to Cavour a project for an
alliance between France and Piedmont in which everything
was taken into account : arrangements for military co-opera-

tion; agreement upon political objects; the marriage of Prince Napoleon with the eldest daughter of Victor Emmanuel. Finally, at the end of May, Dr. Conneau arrived in Turin to inform Cavour that Napoleon III wished to discuss Italian affairs privately with him, and that the interview should take place in the middle of July at Plombières, where the Emperor intended to take the waters.

Cavour felt that he had attained his end. It is pleasant to picture him in this brilliant moment in his career when he appeared as a fine flower of the human race. Forty-seven years of age, physically robust, with a spirited and mischievous eye, a mouth at once sensual and ironic, humorous, open-hearted, observant, a clear thinker, and a precise and finished speaker, a debater feared for his command of brilliant and irresistible repartee, animated by an untiring energy that was yet so well-disciplined and distributed that he even found time in the midst of his multifarious activities to pursue his amours, and, above all, by an unshakable optimism and courage that enabled him with smiling countenance to face the world and shoulder the heavy responsibilities that were thrust upon him. Such was the man as he appeared when talking with his colleagues in the Chamber, or in the anterooms of the Carignan Palace, or when spending his evening with his niece, the exhilarating Marchioness Alfieri, or when taking his daily after-luncheon stroll through the arcades of the Rue du Po. The shopkeepers who encountered him in his walk used to say to one another: "Ah! there is good news to-day. Papa Camillo is rubbing his hands!"

IV

On 11 July Cavour set out for Plombières.   In accordance with a preconcerted plan he shrouded his journey in the deepest secrecy.   It was indeed a conspiracy rather than a conference that he was to attend.   The King and La Marmora, the Minister for War, alone shared in the secret. Alleging that he was in urgent need of rest, Cavour gave out that he was leaving for Switzerland, where he intended to spend a fortnight with his de La Rive cousins.   He was filled with impatience, he declared, " to breathe in peace the pure mountain air far from the society of those who thought of nothing but politics ! "   That he might the better conceal the real purpose of his journey he wrote to his Parisian friend, Madame de Circourt : " If only I were free to direct my steps in accordance with my desires, I would ask to share your hospitality at Bougival.   But chained as I am to the car of politics, I cannot deviate from certain paths.   Moreover, if I were to enter France at a time when the diplomats are uselessly conferring in an endeavour to find a solution to a problem which they have themselves rendered insoluble, my journey would become the subject of all sorts of comment."

After a brief stay at Mont Cenis, where a beginning had been made of boring the tunnel, Cavour arrived at Pressinge, in the neighbourhood of Geneva, where his cousins lived. Taking great care to make the fact of his presence there as public as possible, he even permitted himself to be fêted by the cantonal Government.   Outwardly calm and indifferent, his inward anxiety can be glimpsed in a letter he wrote to La Marmora : " The drama reaches its close. Pray Heaven that it may inspire me and save me from any error at this supreme moment. My inborn petulance and easy self-confidence have not been able to free me from great anxiety." One fine morning he slipped away from Pressinge, armed with a false passport, and travelled by Bâle and Strasburg to Plombières, where he arrived on 20 July at nine o'clock at night. The season was at its height, and every hotel was filled to overflowing with a fashionable crowd. At last he found a lodging in a small chemist's shop. There, amidst the paraphernalia of red and green bottles, in a feverish anxiety, he kept his vigil.

Next day, at eleven o'clock, he entered the Emperor's study. The two conspirators stood face to face. Of what passed between them there exists no record except the report which Cavour wrote for Victor Emmanuel immediately before his departure from Plombières. Hence the following narrative depends upon the sole witness of that report.

After a few preliminary observations, the Emperor revealed his entire plan. He was determined—so he said —to support Piedmont whole-heartedly in a war with Austria, provided a reasonable *casus belli* could be found which would arouse the sympathy of France and all Europe. Where, and in what way, could such a *casus belli* be found ? Surprised by the audacity no less than by the unexpectedness of such a question, which surpassed all his fondest hopes, Cavour was visibly disconcerted and stammered a reply. The Emperor came to his rescue. It would require the pen of a Machiavelli or a Saint-Simon to do justice to the

11

scene that followed. Recovering his self-possession, Cavour resumed the theme he had so brilliantly handled in the Congress of Paris : that is to say, the illegal domination exercised by Austria in Italy, the prolonged occupation of the Romagna, etc. To this the Emperor objected that since these complaints had not been deemed sufficient to warrant the intervention of France and Great Britain in 1856, they could not now constitute a *casus belli*, and he added : " Moreover, as my troops occupy Rome, I cannot demand that Austria evacuates Ancona and Bologna." Cavour at once admitted the justice of this objection, although he did his utmost to win the Emperor's acceptance for it, since " a good and sufficient cause " for war could not always be found. With the Emperor at his side, Cavour rapidly surveyed the various Italian States, and, when he had traversed the whole Peninsula, he placed his finger upon the district in which a conflagration might be started with the greatest ease : the tiny principality of Massa and Carara, which belonged to the despotic Francis V, Duke of Modena. Here an insurrection could be fomented ; the inhabitants would appeal to Piedmont for aid ; the Turin Government would address a provocative note to the ducal Government ; the Duke would reply with his accustomed insolence ; Victor Emmanuel would then occupy Massa ; Austria would mobilise, and war would be declared ! In a piquant scene the two crafty plotters proceeded to elaborate their plan. " We should still have to deal," said the Emperor, " with two serious difficulties in Italy : the Pope and the King of Naples. I will deal with them : with the former lest he raise the French Catholics against me ; with the latter in order to have on my side the sympathies of Russia, with whom it is a point of honour to protect King Ferdinand." Cavour was quick to reply : " To deal with the Pope will be a simple matter. One must leave him in possession of the City of the Apostle and the Patrimony of St. Peter on condition that he gives up the Romagna, for that beautiful district has suffered greatly under the pontifical regime. As to the King of Naples, in his case the task will be even simpler. One need not trouble about him since a chance revolution would hurl him from his throne ! " Satisfied with Cavour's reply, the Emperor went on to consider the form in which the political results of the war should be embodied. He admitted readily that it would be necessary to expel the Austrians entirely from the Peninsula and " not to leave them in possession of a foot of territory on this side of the Alps and the Isonzo." When that had been done, how was Italy to be reorganised ? The problem was one of peculiar difficulty and complexity. Only after prolonged discussion did the two conspirators arrive at the solution which follows. A great kingdom of Upper Italy must be constituted, stretching along the whole valley of the Po, which would unite under the sceptre of Victor Emmanuel Piedmont, Lombardy, Venetia, Emilia, and the Romagna. The Pope should retain the Eternal City and its environs. The remainder of the Papal States and Tuscany should be erected into a kingdom of Central Italy. As for the kingdom of Naples, it should be left alone for the time being. Then these four States should be formed into a confederation on the model of the German Confederation, and the presidency should be offered to Pius IX as some consolation for being deprived of the best part of his territories. In agreeing to this scheme Napoleon made no secret of his desire to give the Neapolitan throne to Prince Murat and that of Tuscany to the good Duchess of Parma, since he had no wish " to appear as the persecutor of the Bourbons."

The future of Italy having thus been determined, and having nothing further to offer Cavour, Napoleon demanded, as a recompense for what he had given, that Victor Emmanuel should cede Nice and Savoy to him. Cavour tactfully sought to avoid this demand. In former days the province had had many ties with France ; nevertheless it was the birthplace of the Piedmontese dynasty, the House of Savoy, and it would be a heavy sacrifice on Victor Emmanuel's part to sever his ancestral ties with it. He objected to the cession of Nice still more warmly : " By their origin, their language, and their customs, the people of Nice are one with the Italian family. To annex them to France would be a violation of the principle of nationality ! " For a time the Emperor remained silent, twisting his moustache. Then he said : " Bah ! It is a minor matter. We can settle it later."

Territorial questions having been disposed of, the problem of the conduct of the war remained. Napoleon thought that Austria would never give up her Italian territories " until she felt the sword's point at her heart." Hence it would be necessary to carry the war into the Empire, and even up to the gates of Vienna. For this a great army of 300,000 men would be required, of which France would contribute two-thirds. Finally, mention was made of the attitude of the various European Powers in the event of a war, and the Emperor declared that he could count on the sympathy of England, the strict neutrality of Prussia, and the moral support of Russia.

The discussion had now lasted for some four hours. The Emperor terminated the audience by requesting Cavour to return in an hour's time to continue the discussion while taking a drive with him. At the appointed hour Napoleon and his guest entered a phaeton in which they drove through the wooded valleys of the Vosges. When they had left Plombières a short distance behind them, the Emperor broached a delicate subject : the marriage of Prince Napoleon with Princess Clotilda, eldest daughter of King Victor Emmanuel. Without hesitation he declared that he attached a great value to the marriage. The political conspiracy now turned into a comedy, which, as may be imagined, infinitely delighted Cavour's malicious nature. In reply to the pressing overtures of the Emperor, Cavour said that the King would doubtless have no insurmountable objection to the marriage. But, on the other hand, the Princess Clotilda was very young—indeed, scarcely fifteen ! Then, too, there was the character of Prince Napoleon, his passions and lack of morals—at least, so it was said. The Emperor sought to excuse his notorious cousin : " He is better than his reputation ! Certainly, he is spirited, impetuous, censorious, loving contradiction and paradox. I have often had to complain of him, but he is good-hearted and at bottom seriously minded. The ability with which he presided over the Exhibition of 1855 testifies to his possession of this latter characteristic. While his faithfulness to his friends, and even to his mistresses, is a proof of his goodness of heart. Believe me! a heartless man would not have left Paris in the midst of the carnival season in order to pay a last visit to the dying Rachel; and, too, when their love-affair had been ended for four years!"

It was impossible for Cavour not to be touched by this portrait. Not that he was unprepared for the Emperor's insistence, since for a long time past he had known through Bixio that the marriage with Princess Clotilda was no less desired in the Palais-Royal than in the Tuileries. He had in his pocket the consent of Victor Emmanuel, who was prepared to give up his daughter, if Napoleon made his doing so a condition *sine qua non* of an alliance. But affairs had gone too well that morning, the alliance was already sufficiently well assured, to render it necessary for Cavour to play his last card. He reserved the decision for the King, in his capacity of tender father not wishing to oppose the feelings of the youthful princess. Invariably kind-hearted and even generous when personal issues were at stake, Napoleon forbore to insist; he contented himself instead with emphasising how greatly it would gratify him to unite the House of France with that of Savoy by this marriage.

The afternoon wore on and the shadows lengthened on the sides of the wooded hills. The distant summits of the Vosges turned to purple in the dying rays of the setting sun. The time had come to return to Plombières, and to part. When the phaeton stopped before the Imperial villa, Napoleon, taking his guest's hand, said to him in bidding him farewell: " Trust in me as I trust in you." Cavour returned to the chemist's shop, rapidly wrote some notes of his interview, and, after a short sleep, left by the first train for Strasburg.

Cavour left Plombières in a very different manner from that in which he had arrived. He came, walking furtively, with his hat pulled down over his eyes; he left with head erect, a swinging step, a joyful countenance, and a frank, open look. He had thrown off his disguise and torn up his false passport. It was no longer the Signor Giuseppe Benso who travelled; it was " His Excellency Count Camille Cavour, Minister for Foreign Affairs of His Majesty King Victor Emmanuel II." And, despite the many urgent reasons demanding his return to the King, it was not to Turin that he went; on the contrary, it was to the most brilliant and cosmopolitan watering-place in Germany—to Baden, where he knew he would meet with the Regent of Prussia, the King of Würtemberg, Grand Duchess Helena of Russia, and numerous royalties, princes, diplomats, politicians, financiers, and journalists. A brilliant idea had prompted him to this step— an astute idea that did greater credit to his farsightedness than to his sense of honour: the idea of compromising at once his illustrious ally, of compromising him before the whole of Europe, so that it would be impossible for him to gainsay himself, or go back upon his engagements. He knew Napoleon III too well not to expect from him hesitations, delays, regrets, subterfuges, disloyalties, denials, and changes of front. Now, however, in a few days, all Europe would learn that Cavour's visit to Plombières had been undertaken on the express invitation of the Emperor, and that a pact had been concluded between Piedmont and France.

Before they had set out on their drive the Emperor, with

a shrewd smile, had remarked to his guest: " A telegram from Walewski has just been handed to me. Do you know what it contains ? The news of your presence in Plombières ! My police are well informed." In thus speaking Napoleon III never thought that he was ratifying in advance one of the severest condemnations which History has passed upon him. That he took it upon himself, unknown to his ministers, and without the advice or assistance of anyone, to enter into a negotiation with the representative of a small State in which he staked nothing less than the future of France and all the fruits of years of political endeavour—this it is that has earned him the condemnation of History. The greatest monarchs, and even those who were most filled with the consciousness of their own power and most jealous of their kingly rights, have not thought it degrading to take the counsel of other men. Louis XIV never concealed anything from Lionne or Louvois, Pomponne or Torcy. History records with what industry, lofty conception of kingly duty, and scrupulousness he sought to inform himself about affairs in which his pride was deeply engaged, as in the long and tedious deliberations over which he presided in 1700 before permitting the Duc d'Anjou to accept the crown of Spain. Despite his fiery genius and impetuous temperament, Napoleon I never took a grave decision until he had first discussed it with competent advisers. True, he frequently ignored their advice. But he never neglected to survey the ground before he launched an attack. The only monarch besides Napoleon III who sought to justify his schemes by occult means was Louis XV. Moreover, the " Secret du Roi "—that odious system of espionage and lies, equivocation and intrigue—was frequently carried on by worthless agents.

A desire for truth requires the historian to ask whether the interview at Plombières took place exactly as Cavour reported to Victor Emmanuel, or whether he did not colour his narrative to make it fit in with his own ideas. In default of any other witness than this report, how is it possible to know what really passed between the two conspirators? But did not the events that followed bear out the statements of Cavour? If the narrative as a whole is to be regarded as trustworthy, an aspect of it deserves comment : Napoleon III's readiness to desert the two monarchs whom he had declared himself as specially ready to answer for—the Pope and the King of Naples. It is easy to understand his willingness to sacrifice " the tyrant of the Two Sicilies," notwithstanding the interest displayed in that monarch's welfare by Alexander II, for he hoped *in petto* to replace him by his cousin Prince Murat. But Pius IX !—Pius IX, whom he had so recently implored to come to Paris to crown him ; Pius IX, the sponsor of his son ; Pius IX, the mystic Pius IX who in promulgating the doctrine of the Immaculate Conception had earned for himself not only the veneration but also the affection of the whole Catholic world : how could Napoleon III consent to deprive him of four-fifths of his estates without a single word of protest? How did it come about that he did not perceive any of the insoluble problems that the Roman Question would continually set before him until the last day of his reign, the eve of Sedan? It can only be supposed that he was out-manœuvred, cajoled by the eloquence of his interrogator, by the swift, lucid, spirited, incisive, pressing, and unconstrained argument of which Cavour was so great a master.

Among the declarations attributed to Napoleon III by Cavour, yet another deserves to be noticed. How could the Emperor be certain that neither England nor Prussia nor Russia would oppose his war with Austria—would be content to leave the road to Vienna open before him? The answer is that he believed it in all sincerity. On the evening of Solferino he was cruelly disillusioned.

Viewed from the standpoint of the Italian cause, what judgment must be passed upon Cavour? Or was his conduct wholly free from criticism? Were his arguments and his sallies impeccable? In this duel in which his adversary put up so poor a defence, could he not press home his advantages to the full? By many of his countrymen he has been censured because, at the outset, he did not lay down as a fundamental axiom the unity of Italy; because he agreed that the Peninsula should be divided into four States, united in a confederacy under the presidency of the Pope. But, in truth, in so acting he was adopting the wisest course. When Cavour found himself alone in a *tête-à-tête* with a providential Cæsar, what was his predominant concern? To secure the French alliance. For he was not negotiating on equal terms. Napoleon III ruled over an empire of more than 36,000,000 inhabitants that could place in the field an army of 400,000 men; Cavour, on his side, represented a small kingdom of 5,000,000 inhabitants with an army of 50,000. Besides, in July 1858, the conception of Italian unity had as yet not developed sufficiently to warrant its being regarded as a political force. While such a consideration had little or no effect upon pioneers and theorists like Tosti, Mazzini, Balbo, and Gioberti, the practical genius of Cavour forbade his concerning himself with schemes until the moment when they had become realisable in practice.

Then, too, the opportunity came to him to negotiate alone with a man who had never been able to weigh the implications of his actions. If he had been imprudent enough to reveal to Napoleon III that he was in train to create at the foot of the Alps, even on the flank of France, a great unified nation of 28,000,000 inhabitants, stretching between two seas and capable of vast expansion, would the dreamer not have waked from his dream? In his report to Victor Emmanuel Cavour reveals his basic idea : the creation of a kingdom of Upper Italy is but the necessary prelude to national unity. " Sovereign over the richest and strongest State in Italy, Your Majesty will in reality be ruler over the whole Peninsula."

Could the cession of Nice and Savoy, the amputation of a limb from Piedmont, have been avoided? It was in this very particular that the practical genius of Cavour displayed itself to the fullest. Pope Julius II had inscribed on the pontifical standard the words : *Italia extero liberanda* (" Italy can only be delivered by a foreigner "). Charles Albert, on the contrary, had said : *L'Italia farà da se* (" Italy must be her own deliverer "). Between these two contradictory mottoes Cavour had to make a choice : he chose that of Julius II. All his study and experience had convinced him that without external aid the enfranchisement of Italy was unrealisable ; and for this aid Italy would have to pay. If she were to accept a gratuitous service from France, she would remain indefinitely under French tutelage ; she would only exchange one dependence for another. Briefly, in the interview at Plombières, Cavour once again showed that at every turn in the game he possessed a sense of what was practicable and necessary. When an unhoped-for opportunity presented itself before him, he had the ability to seize and use it to the full—to seize and use it with the ready audacity of a man who knows that Fortune is like a capricious woman whose gifts should be taken the moment they are offered without giving her time for reflection.

CHAPTER VI

THE MARRIAGE OF PRINCESS CLOTILDA WITH PRINCE NAPOLEON

CHAPTER VI

THE MARRIAGE OF PRINCESS CLOTILDA WITH PRINCE
NAPOLEON

I

ON 31 July Cavour returned to Turin. His cheerful face, his sparkling eyes, and the radiance which seemed to emanate from his entire personality were sufficient to prove the success which he had just achieved at Plombières. Without wasting a moment he set to work. First of all, according to his custom, he mapped out in his brain the general lines of his programme, and arranged all the pieces on his chessboard.

Naturally the King was the first to whom he confided his plans; he found him, as he had expected, full of enthusiasm, already impatient to mount his horse and rush into battle. His simple and straightforward mind, which, however, was not lacking in subtlety, appreciated very justly the new situation : " Above all do not let us fall into the hands of the diplomatists ! To gain our ends, guns are necessary, and as soon as possible ! "

One of the questions discussed tentatively at Plombières and on which Cavour had made no definite engagement, lessened the joy of Victor Emmanuel : the marriage of Princess Clotilda with Prince Napoleon. The pressing demand of the Emperor had not taken Victor Emmanuel unawares; he had foreseen it; he had even acquiesced in it in advance. Now the hour had come to undertake a definite engagement, to pronounce an irrevocable sentence. The more the King thought it over, the more repugnant did the marriage appear to him. For a political aim he was to deliver over his daughter, whom he adored, to a man twenty years her senior! To a man who did not even belong to one of the old reigning families! What a dislike he felt for him! Everyone was agreed that he was an egoist; that his morals were scandalous; that he was addicted to insulting fits of rage; that there was nothing generous, nothing chivalrous in his character; that his conduct before Sevastopol had been pitiable, and that he had deserved to be brought before a court-martial; finally, and this was a still more serious fault, that he displayed a cynical impiety, a blasphemous and provocative atheism. Would it not be a sacrilege to hand over body and soul to such a man a child who was full of purity, candour, nobility, and devotion?

The anguished revolt of the father's conscience was met by Cavour with arguments in which he urged those reasons of State that amounted for him to a "categorical imperative." True, he said, the marriage is not an indispensable condition of the Alliance, and, even if it does not take place, the Alliance may none the less be concluded. Would this Alliance, however, on which the whole fate of Italy depends, have the same value in the one case as in the other? Certainly it would not, for by the refusal of Princess Clotilda's hand the susceptibilities of Napoleon III would be mortally wounded. " I know the Emperor well ; one of his distinctive traits is the constancy of his feelings ; he never forgets a service, and he never forgives an injury.   He would, therefore, bear a lasting grudge against you, Sire, for having wounded him in his dynastic pride. . . . As for Prince Napoleon, do you think he would accept such an affront calmly ? You would have in him henceforward an implacable enemy. Would not the rank which he holds in the Imperial family, his activity, and his talents combined with the affection, or rather the weakness, which the Emperor has for him, afford him only too many opportunities of making us feel his hatred.   In any case, I declare to Your Majesty with the deepest conviction that to accept the Alliance and refuse the marriage would be an immense political mistake which might bring down upon our country the greatest misfortunes."

Abandoning reasons of State, the subtle Minister next sought to calm the father's disquietude and repugnance. " Will Your Majesty permit me to review the question no longer with the impassiveness of a diplomat but with the absolute and affectionate devotion which I have vowed to you ? Can it be said that the marriage of Princess Clotilda with Prince Napoleon would be unsuitable ? He is not a king, it is true, but he is the first Prince of the Blood Royal of the first Empire in the world, and he is only separated from the throne by a child of two years old.   Again, it is true that he does not belong to an old reigning house, but his father will leave to him the most glorious name of modern times, and through his mother, the Princess of Würtemberg, he is connected with the most illustrious houses in Europe. The nephew of the doyen of kings, the cousin of the Emperor of Russia, cannot be called a parvenu whom one cannot marry without shame. . . . I now come to objections of a more intimate character, to the objections founded on the personal character of the Prince, and his scandalous reputation. I will repeat to you, Sire, what the Emperor told me at Plombières with accents of perfect sincerity : 'Prince Napoleon is worth more than his reputation.' Thrown when he was very young into the whirlpool of revolution, he has let himself be carried away by extremist opinions which have been the cause of his making so many enemies. He has, however, become more moderate in his opinions ; although, and this does him every honour, he has remained faithful to the liberal principles of his youth while renouncing the danger of putting them into practice ; in fact, he has braved the anger of his cousin rather than disavow his friends of former times who have fallen into disgrace. No, in truth, he is not bad at heart. . . . If Your Majesty deigns to reflect on the considerations which I have just submitted to you, I venture to flatter myself that you will recognise that you can, as a father, consent to this marriage which the supreme interests of State, the future of your House, of Piedmont, and of Italy counsel you to authorise." So spoke Cavour ; in such manner was the ingenious Ulysses wont subtly to mix " words of force with words of honey."

Not knowing what to reply, the King ended by yielding ; but only on condition that he was not asked to deal this blow to his daughter himself. He could not even bring his words to an end ; both his heart and his voice failed him. He, therefore, charged Cavour to notify the Princess of the fatal decision, but still wished that it should remain absolutely secret until the very eve of the public betrothal. The odious formalities were to be shortened as much as possible.

Once he had made his paternal sacrifice, Victor Emmanuel's mind was filled with brave thoughts, bright hopes, fearless confidence, and an unconquerable and radiant firmness of spirit. Henceforth he entered fully into his historic rôle; he personified to a marvellous degree the hero whom Machiavelli had already foretold, invoking in him all his desires. " May Italy after such long waiting, after her long suspense, see her liberator appear at last. Words fail me to express with what love, what fidelity, what reverence, what tears of joy, he would be greeted in all our provinces, which have suffered so much from foreign hands. Would not the gates of all our cities open before him ? What Italian would refuse to obey him ? With what transports of joy would our common fatherland rally to his standard ? "

Regarded in their living reality rather than in a symbolical aspect, the features of Victor Emmanuel greatly resemble those of Henri IV. In both are seen the vigorous stamp of character, nobility of feeling, high conception of royal dignity, and, in addition, all the warlike virtues, courage, endurance, audacity, and spirit. It must be admitted that were this parallel carried still further, the Béarnais would triumph over Victor Emmanuel in the breadth of his political views, his flashes of genius, his art of managing men, and, finally, in the elegance of his demeanour, the outstanding and attractive grace of his wit.

Having thus gained for all his ideas the approval of the King, which was to prove an invaluable support in the

future, Cavour embarked resolutely on the first article of
his programme—military preparations. General La Marmora, as Minister for War, was indeed the right man in the
right place, being an administrator rather than a strategist
and possessing in a very high degree a sense of organisation
and of distribution and co-ordination. The plan was put
into action immediately, and, within a very short time, in
spite of the precautions taken for secrecy, work in the arsenals,
powder-magazines, and fortresses became so intensive that
the Austrian spies throughout the country began to send in
warnings.

The second article of the programme which Cavour had
traced out was not less difficult to realise, for to the practical
difficulties were added difficulties of a moral nature ; it
became a question of combining every element in order
that at a suitable moment the whole of Italy would rise like
one man against its hated masters. The instrument for
this general explosion was already in being. Cavour had
forged it himself a year before with the ready aid of the
great revolutionaries Pallavicino, La Farina, and Garibaldi :
it was the Italian Nationalist Society of which the hidden
ramifications spread from Turin to the borders of the
Adriatic, Calabria, and even as far as Sicily.

The next thing to be done was to draw up a plan of
campaign in which the least details were provided for, in
which the chiefs and their principal assistants were designated
by name, in which the dates, the objectives, the means, the
subsidies, the pass-words, the meeting-places, and the routes
were precisely determined. In order to set this machine
in action, forming as it did the greatest conspiracy known

to History, Cavour shut himself up every morning from daybreak with La Farina.

In thus viewing this Minister of a long-established monarchy conspiring against other monarchs by Divine Right, and organising conspiracies, mutinies, aggressions, felonies, and revolts, in their countries, it is impossible to repress a smile in recalling the aphorism of the grave Guizot, that "nothing noble or durable can be founded on violence or disorder, for revolution is as fatal to the greatness which it seeks to establish as it is to that which it overthrows."

On 19 October Cavour and his coadjutor had completed their plan of campaign. The first step was to take the form of a riot which should break out at Massa and Carrara in the night of 30 April 1859. Under cover of the riot a band of daring men were to seize the authorities, take possession of the arsenal, and disarm the garrison. Immediately afterwards Garibaldi and three hundred volunteers were to disembark at Lérici near Spezia ; after crossing the Apennines by forced marches they were to take Parma, Reggio, Modena, and Bologna. Simultaneously, the Lombards and the Venetians were to cut the telegraph wires, destroy the railway lines, and set the military magazines on fire. Thereupon, under pretext of protecting its territories against the surrounding anarchy, the Piedmontese Government was to occupy Massa and Carrara. After this, the Austrian army would cross the Ticino, and France would rush to the help of Piedmont.

In order to secure the successful execution of the plan, Cavour summoned to Turin several patriots from Central

Italy whose courage and discretion inspired him with confidence. Among these were Marco Minghetti and Count Pasolini, both former Ministers of Pius IX in 1848 ; to them Cavour carefully revealed all his preparations. Incredulous at first, and even wondering if he had not gone out of his mind, they left Cavour at last convinced, transformed, and ineffably happy. But, indeed, with men of their social rank and political education Cavour's task was an easy one.

It next became necessary for Cavour, without further delay, to place himself in direct communication with the red-shirted demagogue who had once been solemnly condemned to death by a Piedmontese Court—Garibaldi. On 28 August he sent for him from Capréra, where, in the company of the ocean, the uncouth paladin was pursuing his ardent and solitary dreams. When these two men, so different and with nothing in common but their patriotism, had opened their hearts to each other, and, being agreed on every point, had cordially grasped each other's hands, it is not too much to say that the foundation-stone of Italian unity was laid for all time by the union of the people with the monarchy, and by the definite rallying of the revolutionary party to the House of Savoy.

Cavour saw that the value of this gesture, destined as it was to exercise an immense influence in the *Risorgimento*, could be added to by a process of inversion. While the revolutionary forces were working in the Peninsula for the profit of the Italian cause, it was necessary that they also should work with no less energy to shake the power of the Habsburgs on the banks of the Danube, to stir up Hungary into insurrection. How could Austria maintain a great military effort south of the Alps, if she were struck in the back ?

Cavour therefore entered into secret negotiations with one of the principal leaders of the Magyar insurrection of 1848, the brilliant disciple and companion of the great Kossuth, General Klapka. Towards the end of September he sent for him to come to Turin, and said to him : " I have brought back from my journey to Plombières a conviction that the Eastern Question will soon lead to conflict between France and Austria. Piedmont is preparing for this eventuality. You Hungarians must prepare also, for you are no less interested than we are." They soon came to an understanding to awake in the soul of Hungary the epic memories of 1848, to stir up trouble in the towns and in the country, to encourage desertion from the Hungarian regiments, and, indeed, to form, in the army of Piedmont, a Magyar legion of which Klapka himself would take command.

Never had the activity of Cavour been so intense. All who came into contact with him at this time affirm that he was the leader in everything, and that it was impossible to imagine the immensity of his capacity for work. He took in hand the motive power, all the levers of command : he was, simultaneously, President of the Council, Minister for Foreign Affairs, Minister for War, Minister for Marine, and Minister for Public Works. He did not seem in any way exhausted by this volume of work, so regular, precise, and vigorous was his self-discipline.

Rising at 4 o'clock in the morning (for this was the hour when he received La Farina and his secret agents), he breakfasted at 9 o'clock on a piece of bread, two eggs, and a cup of tea. At about 10 o'clock he walked briskly to his official office, where he read dispatches, scanned the newspapers, and questioned his assistants ; he then went to see the King, attended the Council of Ministers, the Senate, and the Chamber of Deputies, held conferences with the General Staff, and with financial commissions. At 4 o'clock came diplomatic audiences. Immediately afterwards he allowed himself a few moments of repose at the house of his niece the Marchioness Alfieri. At 6 o'clock he returned to the Palazzo Cavour, where he dined alone, and enjoyed a short sleep in an armchair. Then, again, until midnight intensive work. Rarely has the human machine supported such an enormous effort, regulated so perfectly. One day, about the year 1825, Eckermann asked Goethe by what constituent elements the genius of Napoleon could be explained, and the illustrious old man replied : " Very little sleep, very little food, a will which never ceased to act, a mind in which the light was never extinguished for an instant." Is there any other explanation of the genius of Cavour ?

II

In spite of all his labours and the attention and ardour which he devoted to them, there was one thought which never left him. What was Napoleon III doing ? Was he also preparing to play his rôle in the drama which was so soon to be staged ? Was the enigmatic and taciturn dreamer still pursuing the same dream ?

In order to keep a better hold on his secret informers and also to encourage the over-cautious Villamarina, he sent a young officer, Chevalier Nigra, to Paris. This young man had just started his career in diplomacy, and his agreeable manners, finesse, and readiness had impressed Cavour so favourably that after attaching him to his person he soon made of him his most intimate helper.

It was through this able emissary that all the secret communications were to pass henceforth between Paris and Turin. First of all he was to gain the absolute confidence of the Emperor and Prince Napoleon. He was to succeed in insinuating himself into the good graces of the Empress, who, however, did not hide her hostility to the ambitions of Piedmont. Better still, he was to find the means of interesting the woman while speaking to the sovereign and to discover a means of moving that heart at once so irreproachable, so cold, so arid, and so poor in tender memories. As he did not fail to keep his chief regularly informed of what was going on, he received from him this astute reply : " Your conversation with the Empress has pleased me very much. Evidently she wishes to captivate you. Let her do it. Do not be too much of a Joseph. In the long run her influence against us could be very injurious. You must neglect *nothing* to make her favourable to us. Keep on telling her that the Italians find her charming. In any case, it seems to me that you have no need of lessons and that you know how to make the most of the situation quite in the manner of Richelieu or Metternich. I am keeping to myself what you have written and what you will write to me on this delicate subject. Your letters will be sealed and returned to you if any accident occurs to me."

Cavour could not do otherwise than congratulate himself

on all that he heard from Paris in the autumn of 1858. Whatever the source of his information, it all tended to show the fidelity of the Emperor to the Pact of Plombières.

On 4 August Napoleon III went to Cherbourg with the Empress to celebrate the completion of the port and to preside at the unveiling of a statue of Napoleon I.

Queen Victoria and Prince Albert came to greet him. The interview was full of cordiality. The bitter controversies which had so greatly prejudiced the relations of France and England after the Orsini outrage seemed to be forgotten. An able speech from the Emperor produced an excellent effect not only in London but also in the whole of Europe. " The stronger a government is, the more moderation it displays in its councils, the more justice in its resolutions. One cannot risk the peace of a country to satisfy empty pride or to acquire temporary popularity. A government that depends on the will of the people is not the slave of any party, it does not make war except when forced to do so to defend the honour or the great interests of the peoples. Let us then continue to develop in peace the varied resources of France ; let us invite foreigners to visit our industries ; let them come as friends and not as rivals," etc.

In this peaceful speech, in this appeal to concord, industry, and wisdom, who could have suspected inimical undercurrents ? But Cavour did not allow himself to be disquieted by such a tone, for he understood, as only he could understand, what was meant by the allusion to the " great interests of the peoples."

As soon as the festival at Cherbourg was over the Emperor continued his game of dissimulation. He left for

Brittany, where he had not shown himself since his accession. In official circles a certain amount of nervousness was felt regarding a journey in a province that still made a parade of legitimist opinions, and passed for the impregnable citadel of the white flag. During the progress of the sovereigns, however, the population flocked with priest and banner to see them.

The country of La Rochejaquelein and of Cadoudal, the classic land of the Chouans, showed itself more Bonapartist than any other district of France. For the last act of this ingenious scenario Napoleon III had wished to celebrate the festival of 15 August at Sainte-Anne d'Auray. The enthusiasm of the Bretons knew no bounds when they saw the Emperor prostrate himself before the altar of their favourite saint. The bishops, the priests, the Government officials, the mayors, rivalled each other in eloquence in praise of "the new Charlemagne who, after restoring the Sovereign-Pontiff to his throne, has become the valiant defender of the Papacy in the nineteenth century." As at Cherbourg, so now no suspicions were aroused that the Emperor had just entered into an understanding with Piedmont to strip Pius IX of four-fifths of his dominions and to begin a war whose ultimate consequences would be the destruction of the Temporal Power.

Once again Cavour did not allow himself to be disturbed. He had practised too long the gospel of Machiavelli not to remember the axiom of that great professor of deceit: "A Prince should always conceal his designs and march towards his object by roads which appear to lead in the opposite direction."

With regard to Walewski, Napoleon III dissimulated so successfully that the simple-minded Minister was taking his ease with a feeling of the greatest security. On 22 August, while talking to Hübner, he congratulated himself sanctimoniously on the wise dispositions which the Emperor was taking, especially as far as Italian affairs were concerned. " M. de Cavour," he said, " is exploiting in the newspapers his visit to Plombières and is using every effort to give it a significance which it does not possess. The Emperor spoke to me about it at Cherbourg : *An attempt is being made to make it believed that I have hostile intentions against Austria. Nothing could be more false ! Of course, I have great sympathy for Piedmont and also a love for Italy, and I shall always continue to show signs of my sympathy to the Italians, but within certain limits and never to the point of compromising the preservation of peace.*"

His peace of mind was not shaken when towards the end of September he suddenly learned that the Emperor was sending Prince Napoleon as envoy to Warsaw, to carry greetings to the Tsar Alexander II. " A simple mission of ceremonial and routine," he declared to all the diplomats who asked him questions about this unexpected journey. " What proves beyond all doubt that the Prince is not charged with any political negotiations, is the fact that Montebello, the French ambassador, is not accompanying him." He would have been astounded if he could have read the letter which the Imperial envoy received from Cavour on his return from Poland : " I thank Your Highness for the kind messages which you have been good enough to send me by M. Nigra. I have been profoundly touched by them, as for a long time I have felt respectful sympathy with Your Highness. Now I feel more than ever attached and grateful to you for the striking part which you have taken in the great enterprise that is to assure the independence of Italy and Piedmont. The Warsaw Mission which Your Imperial Highness has carried out with ability so rare will contribute immensely to the success of this enterprise. The help of the Tsar, even when it is confined to preventing the interference of Germany in our affairs, will, in my opinion, secure to us a favourable result for the war. In obtaining this help for us, Your Highness has rendered the greatest of services to our cause." This letter opens a new phase in the conspiracy hatching between Paris and Turin. It marks the entry on the scene of Prince Napoleon. His familiarity with the Emperor, his rare gifts of intelligence and eloquence, his fascinating manner and physical charm, his imposing appearance, his outbursts of anger and pride, his republican airs, his insolent contempt for hierarchies and official ceremonies, his fevered desire to play a great historic rôle, his pretence of being the only true interpreter of Napoleonic ideas, his passionate love of Italy, his hatred of the Habsburgs, of Pius IX, and of the priests, his hatred of the Empress, in fact, all the powerful nature of this *déclassé* Cæsar rendered him a marvellous reinforcement to Cavour's plans at the most critical moment.

III

Henceforth the preliminaries of the drama moved on apace, especially the negotiations for that " treaty of offensive and defensive alliance " for which the basis had been laid at Plombières. Everything was carried out in the most profound secrecy by Victor Emmanuel and Cavour, on the one side, and the Emperor and his cousin on the other; Nigra, by means of constant journeys, made an exchange of views possible.

On 24 December, except for a few details of phraseology, the agreement was complete. The signatures alone were wanting. By the political treaty, to which were added military and financial conventions, France undertook to support Piedmont if she were attacked by Austria, the essential object of the alliance being to set Italy free from Austrian domination; when that had been done, Piedmont was to annex Lombardy, Venetia, the duchies of Parma and Modena, the Legations and the Marches; an independent kingdom was to be set up in the centre of the Peninsula, the authority of the Pope was to be maintained in the province of Rome, and the duchy of Savoy and county of Nice were to be annexed by France.

When the negotiations were at last completed, Napoleon III decided to reveal their existence to his Foreign Minister. In his consternation Walewski uttered a cry of alarm. " Sire, permit my devotion, which you cannot question, the privilege of telling you that you have committed yourself to a fatal course." He thereupon resigned. But an affectionate letter from his sovereign, and perhaps an even more intimate influence, decided him to recall his resignation. He followed his master on his " fatal course."

On 1 January 1859 the Diplomatic Corps in full uniform assembled at the Tuileries to present their homage to the

Emperor Napoleon III. Affecting his most sibylline expression, the Emperor received with ceremonious coldness the compliments of the Papal Nuncio. But when the Austrian ambassador stood before him his eyes suddenly flashed, and in a slow and deliberate voice he uttered these words: " I regret that the relations between our two countries are not as good as formerly. Be good enough, however, to assure the Emperor Francis Joseph that my personal feelings towards him are unchanged." These grave words, uttered under circumstances so solemn on the threshold of the New Year, resounded immediately through the world with a sinister intonation.

It meant war—of course. Public opinion was infatuated with the idea. On the Paris Bourse business ceased. Funds fell, and the most solid securities depreciated.

Scarcely had the public mind become a little calmer when on 11 January a speech from the throne pronounced on the previous day at Turin caused universal consternation. It was still more grave than the words uttered to Hübner. " The year is beginning under a dark sky," said Victor Emmanuel. " Our situation is not without danger, for while we respect the treaties we cannot fail to hear the cry of distress which rises to our ears from so many parts of Italy. Strong in our union, confident in our good faith, we await with caution and resolution the decrees of Providence."

The general disquietude increased throughout Europe, and well-nigh a panic ensued. " They have fired the powder," said Prince Albert, who was awaiting the explosion from one day to the next. With unconcealed joy Cavour wrote to one of his collaborators : " We have at last caught

Austria in a trap from which she can never escape without the firing of cannon."

Two days later there was a new incident : the *Moniteur* announced that Prince Napoleon had left for Turin, accompanied by General Niel. No explanation for the journey was given, but everyone whispered that the Emperor's cousin was going to ask for the hand of Princess Clotilda, and doubtless also to carry out a great political mission.

Matters were soon settled. On 24 January the betrothal was announced. The marriage was to be celebrated in six days.

IV

Since Victor Emmanuel had not the heart to break the news to his daughter of the notable marriage to which he had destined her, it fell to Cavour to carry out this painful task. And it can easily be imagined that he had no conscientious scruples. In a national crisis involving the fate of a whole country, in which thousands of men were about to die, what weight attached to the preferences and doubts of a young girl? It may be said that the extreme youth of the victim should have given him pause, for Clotilda's age was only fifteen years and ten months. Many princesses have been married at that age, even earlier. The age of Princess Elizabeth of Bavaria had been no more than fifteen years and four months when she had married the Emperor Francis Joseph not long before. Cavour did not find it necessary, however, to use his great resources of eloquence to obtain the consent of " Madame Clotilda." He had merely to say that by this marriage she would be doing a great service to the cause of Italy and adding to the glory of her House, for her to consent immediately. Turning to the King, who had just come in, she said : " This marriage cannot be other than suitable for me since you propose it to me. I therefore submit myself without question to your will." Nevertheless she expressed a wish to make the acquaintance of Prince Napoleon before pronouncing the irrevocable word of consent. The satisfaction of this request, reasonable as it was, made necessary the postponement of the marriage. The Emperor agreed without much difficulty, for he was by no means unaware how repugnant from a moral, and how dangerous from a political, point of view would be the coincidence of the signature of the Alliance with the celebration of the marriage, as if the one were the price of the other. Walewski pointed this out to him courageously : " What I said to Your Majesty this morning regarding the expediency of postponing the marriage seems to me to be worthy of serious consideration. The impression that for an exclusively dynastic interest, and to obtain an establishment for a cousin, you are exposing the country to all the calamities of a war, would produce an effect that would be rendered even more deplorable by the fact that this cousin is unpopular with the country. Would it not be better to agree secretly to the marriage while taking the greatest care that the news of it does not leak out before the war ? The marriage could be celebrated immediately after the peace without appearing to be unsuitable."

The formidable cousin, however, would not listen to this point of view, but wished to strike the unexpected note of the double dénouement, fearing that once the Alliance was signed the marriage would pass him by.

This marriage had in fact become for him a sort of haunting hallucination upon which all the ardour of his impulsive and arrogant nature was concentrated. In the first place he had long desired to have a regular establishment which, without interfering in any way with his dissolute caprices, would permit him to maintain his position in the Empire with more luxury and authority. Then how gratifying to his pride in his relations with his cousin if he were admitted by marriage into the most ancient dynasty in Europe! As it was, he was of better birth than Napoleon III, for his mother Catherine had been a Princess of Würtemberg before ascending the throne of Westphalia ; Queen Hortense had been merely a Beauharnais! How much more would he not gain by his marriage—a Princess Clotilda compared to a Montijo! Finally, he, like the Emperor, had his secret dream. A great dream which he confided to none but a few intimates. The independent kingdom which was to be established in the centre of Italy by adding to Tuscany vast fragments of Papal territory ; that kingdom which by its history, monuments, culture, eloquence, and Attic spirit would be the happiest in the Peninsula, he wanted for himself. Before the outbreak of war, he must establish himself upon Italian soil. How could he better achieve this than by an alliance with the House of Savoy ?

V

On his arrival in Turin on 16 January he began to push forward simultaneously and with equal energy the matrimonial and the political negotiation. There was no difficulty whatever about the alliance, for the work of composing the treaty was already well-nigh finished and the final protocols in draft form.

On 24 January one of the Prince's aides-de-camp, Major Ferri-Pisani, brought the treaty of alliance and the accompanying military and financial agreements to Paris. Napoleon III thereupon signed it, and on 26 January the aide-de-camp carried the documents back to Turin, where Victor Emmanuel signed them in his turn on 29 January. The originals, however, bore the date the 12 and 16 December 1858. .This was done at the Emperor's desire : " I was anxious to antedate the documents," he wrote to his cousin, " in order not to give any countenance to those who are saying everywhere that your marriage is a bargain and that it has not been possible to obtain it without making a treaty." The Prince himself was no less active in hurrying on the marriage negotiations.

As for " Madame Clotilda," she soon perceived that opposition was useless, and she therefore gave her consent without any resistance. This Princess, who had scarcely reached a marriageable age, was already remarkable for her energy, firmness, and self-control. Not at all pretty, she carried herself stiffly, and with her Austrian lip, she was Habsburg to the core. To her deep piety she added a fine and balanced intellect. At a glance she had understood the husband destined for her. Like Racine's Iphigénie, she could say : " Et voilà donc l'hymen où j'étais destinée ! " Immediately, however, her religious feelings and a sense of royal tradition took possession of her heart. Without a murmur she consented to a sacrifice that ended only with her life. Bound to a man whose every instinct revolted her, she remained beside him, austere and calm, reserved and mortified, like a Carmelite. She bore with every insult, every humiliation, every violence, he inflicted upon her ; her eyes fixed on the Cross, offering up all her sorrows to the God of love and consolation, and repeating to herself with each fresh trial, " *Paratum est cor meum, Domine !* "

When the news of the marriage was made public at Turin, there was an outburst of indignation. How could the King consent to such a mésalliance, and hand over his daughter to such a man ? The Royal Family was horror-struck ; the Prince of Carignan threw himself at the King's feet to implore him in the name of his mother to spare this disgrace to the House of Savoy. Among the nobility, among the bourgeoisie, among the people themselves, the disapproval was no less violent. The majority of the ladies refused to attend the ball which the President of the Council gave in honour of the Prince.

A telegram from Paris, however, announced that the Emperor had signed the treaty. There was, therefore, no further obstacle to the celebration of the marriage. But an unforeseen difficulty arose. Before receiving the sacrament of marriage the Prince had to make his confession. It is true that he was not expected to make a confession such as is exacted by the canonical law : *humilis et verecunda moerens et lacrymabilis*. The question was one of saving appearances. A way out of the humorous imbroglio was found when an ecclesiastic was sent to him who was famous for his insinuating subtlety. He greeted him with a mocking air and extricated himself from the situation by a piece of buffoonery which would have gained him the applause of Scapin and Figaro.

On 30 January, at ten o'clock in the morning, the Royal Chapel was brilliantly illuminated beneath the famous cupola of Guarini. The Archbishop of Verceil, assisted by four bishops, presided at the ceremony. The bridal pair took their places in front of the altar at a short distance from the King; but while the Princess, looking more white even than her veil, knelt absorbed in worship before God, the Prince saw fit to remain standing with his head held high, his hands resting on his hips, examining with a roving eye the crowd of brilliantly dressed courtiers, or turning to the right and the left with his gaze upturned towards the roof, as though he were studying the structure of the building. He seemed so ignorant of the ceremony itself that several times, for the utterance of the mutual consent, the joining of hands, and the putting on of the ring, the priest was obliged to slip behind him to remind him to carry out these rites. The ordeal, however, was not a long one; by eleven o'clock it was at an end.

On leaving the church, and after a quick change of costume, the newly married pair took the train for Genoa, where they were to embark the next day for Marseilles. Victor Emmanuel and the Royal Family went with them, accompanied by some of the ministers. When, about five o'clock, the procession entered the paved streets of the proud old Ligurian city, the King was saluted by the population with delirious cries of " Vive la guerre ! . . . A bas l'Autriche ! . . . *Vive le roi d'Italie !* " At that moment Cavour's exact memory must have recalled to him the enthusiastic dream which he had pursued eighteen years earlier in this same city of Genoa in the arms of La Giustiniani. Had he not then said, " that he would find it perfectly natural to awake one fine morning *Prime Minister of the Kingdom of Italy* " ?

Scarcely had Prince Napoleon and Princess Clotilda disembarked at Marseilles than Piedmont threw down the gauntlet to Austria. From the tribune Cavour denounced the excessive military activity which was going on in the Kingdom of Lombardy and the massing of forces which was being carried out at Cremona, Plaisance, Pavia, and all along the Ticino. " It is impossible to misunderstand this," he said. " It is an offensive that is in preparation. Piedmont must take immediate steps to be in a position to reply to it." Recalling once again the cries of pain which were rising from the whole of Italy against the dominion of the Habsburgs, he authorised the raising of a loan of 50,000,000 francs for the national defence.

In this sudden demonstration the wily Cavour had in view not only Austria, but still more his new ally, France, for he distrusted Napoleon III. He understood his vacillating and dilatory mentality, and constantly feared some audacity, some sudden change of policy on his part. As when on leaving Plombières he had hastened to compromise him before Europe, so now that the Alliance was concluded he immediately made a striking demonstration in order to commit French policy irrevocably to a belligerent course.

Henceforward he invariably acted towards his Imperial accomplice in this manner, leading him sometimes by surprise and sometimes by intimidation, either by facing him with accomplished facts and thus forcing him to give decisions by anticipating them, or by making him believe that by some impatient gesture he would reveal the understanding existing between them and expose before the world all the secrets of their conspiracy. This method certainly lacked nicety, but collaboration with the Sphinx of the Tuileries was by no means easy.

Cardinal de Retz, whose writings may be read with great profit by those desirous of learning the analysis of character and the management of men, said, speaking of " Monsieur," Duc d'Orléans and Lieutenant-General of the Kingdom : " There was in him a wide separation between slight desire and will, between will and resolution, between resolution and choice of methods, between choice of methods and their application. But what was the most extraordinary of all, he often stopped short in the middle of their application." Napoleon III possessed the same personality. A particular characteristic must, however, be added to it in which the influence of romanticism can be traced : that strange deformity of the mind, that misunderstanding of oneself by which one fabricates an imaginary personality that does not correspond to one's true nature. In this manner a more or less imposing figure is created, possessed of a greater or smaller degree of prestige, holding itself erect as long as it is limited to mechanical manifestations, but crumbling and falling when it is brought into contact with the brutal forces of reality.

In an unfinished study on " Second-rate Cæsars," the terrible Sainte-Beuve had already with great subtlety perceived all that was artificial and spurious, " hollow and electro-plated " in the restorer of the Imperial dynasty. Brought up in the Napoleonic creed, convinced of his Messianic mission, Napoleon III had set himself up as the saviour of France, the arbitrator of Europe, the champion and sword-bearer of oppressed nations. Such a task required for its fulfilment nothing less than one of those great geniuses who have shown themselves as born to make history and to lead peoples. The son of Hortense had in him nothing of the man of action ; neither the clear mind, the straightforward and firm nature, the organising capacity, the strong passions, nor, above all, the equal and stable balance of will. Lymphatic in temperament—a fact that explains his impassive countenance, dull look, swollen eye-lids, monotonous voice, prolonged silences, slow walk, rare gestures, and frequent fits of depression—he took no pleasure except in humanitarian dreams and in generous but indefinite ideas ; he was an idealist, or, better, an ideologist strayed into politics.

Events soon justified the precautions which Cavour had taken in regard to his troublesome ally. On 3 February, Prince Napoleon and Princess Clotilda made their solemn entry into Paris in the midst of a glacial silence, for in the eye of the public their marriage seemed to portend war. On the following day an anonymous pamphlet entitled *Napoleon III and Italy* was distributed among the people. Almost at once it was revealed that this had been inspired, if not actually dictated, by the Emperor. The pamphlet foreshadowed the reorganisation of the Peninsula in a federal system which would exclude all interference on the part of Austria, and the reader's eye was at once caught by the following phrase : " Napoleon I thought it his duty to conquer peoples that he might set them at liberty ; Napoleon III wishes to liberate them without conquest." The pamphlet had an enormous effect surpassing all the author's expectations ; but an effect the opposite of what he desired. Financial, commercial, and industrial circles were absolutely bewildered : shares depreciated, business ceased, the rate of exchange was disturbed and many bankruptcies took place.

In official circles, with the exception of the little half-rebel Court of the Palais-Royal, the criticisms passed all bounds and were expressed with a freedom unknown since 2 December. As was always the case, Persigny was among the most audacious, writing to the Emperor that " Europe and France have accepted you because during nine years they have had faith in your promise to respect treaties. You will lose their confidence if you lead them by your conduct to believe that you will respect them no longer." Walewski expressed himself with no less courage : " The effect of the pamphlet, Sire, is deplorable. On the day on which Your Majesty lets it be known that your policy no longer rests on the maintenance of treaties—on that day you will find the whole world against you. I do not hesitate to affirm that if this ill-timed pamphlet had an official character it would be to-day, and not to-morrow, that Europe would enter into a coalition, not against France itself, but against the Emperor personally. I repeat, Sire, in the present state of public opinion in France and abroad, war is an impossibility ! " Drouyn de Lhuys, who had no longer an opportunity of approaching his Sovereign, went about repeating even before Hübner that " the Emperor has placed himself between the bayonets of the Coalition and the bombs of the conspirators, but the latter will allow him a respite while they are waiting for him to tear up the treaties and to defy Europe." Fould, Baroche, Maupas, Marshal Pélissier and General Fleury expressed themselves in similar terms. Morny went still further. In an address to the Corps Législatif, of which he was the President, he uttered, amidst the applause of the whole assembly, the following significant words : "Religion, philosophy, civilisation, credit, and industry have made peace the chief benefit of modern society ; no longer can the blood of peoples be lightly spilt ; war is the last resource of outraged right or of offended honour. International communications and publicity have created a new force in European affairs with which every Government is bound to reckon—that force is public opinion." Finally, in the Catholic Party, fear and distress were extreme. Mgr de Bonnechose, Archbishop of Rouen, who had been the recipient in 1852 of the first confidences in the affair of the consecration, besought Napoleon III not to break with a policy that had hitherto been so Christian, and not to declare war on Austria with the fatal effect of opening to Piedmont the gates of Rome. Obtaining in return nothing but vague assurances, he uttered this cry of distress : " The Emperor is leading France out of her course. From protector of the Holy See, he is becoming the helper of its enemies. It is an act of madness. I pray God to have pity on us, and to spare us the evils which menace us in menacing the Vicar of Jesus Christ."

Already deeply impressed by the unanimous resistance of French public opinion, the Emperor was soon to see the hostility of Europe directed against him. In London, where nearly everyone was his friend, there was an outcry against his warlike plans.   The English diplomat Henry Greville was only expressing the general indignation when he wrote : " Is it not revolting to think that the peace of the world and the fate of a great part of the human race is in the hands of an unscrupulous adventurer without faith and without honour, who is pursuing only selfish ends, and who, unfortunately, is possessed of enormous power ? "   On this question all political parties were united, Whigs and Tories, Lord Palmerston and Lord Derby, Lord John Russell and Lord Malmesbury.   The movement gained such strength that Queen Victoria wrote to Napoleon III : " Your Majesty must see from the speeches in Parliament what importance England attaches to the preservation of peace.   The deep anxiety of the country on this subject is equalled by my own. To calm the fears of Europe, all that is necessary for you is to affirm that you will respect the treaties.   If anything could increase the horror which I should feel in seeing the outbreak of war, it would be to see Your Majesty pursuing a path in which it would be impossible for England to follow you."   At the same time the Prince Consort sounded the alarm among the German courts, where opinion was only too ready to believe that if the French armies were victorious over the Austrians in Italy, they would immediately hasten to the conquest of the Rhine provinces and Belgium.   The whole of Germany was aroused ; Prussia openly took sides against France, and the astounded Emperor saw forming against him the coalition prophesied by Walewski.

But could not France at least count on the co-operation of Russia ? Was not the pact which Prince Napoleon had

negotiated so mysteriously in Warsaw equivalent to a diplomatic and military alliance which, on the one hand, would
threaten Austria, and, on the other, would compel Germany
to remain quiet? Unfortunately, a negative reply had to
be returned to these questions. Once again the Emperor
was deceived in his calculations; once again his Foreign
Minister, who had been kept ignorant of everything but the
outlines of the negotiations, was compelled to reveal the
truth to him. Walewski was not long in showing him that
" Prince Gortchakoff, finding himself faced by an adversary
as inexperienced as Prince Napoleon, has not hesitated to
make use of him and to abuse his confidence in order to
conclude a one-sided treaty by which the Cabinet of St.
Petersburg obtains our consent to the revision of the Treaty
of Paris without in exchange giving us any guarantee against
a German attack on our Rhine frontier." If, therefore—
his argument proceeded—we make war on Austria, all we
can hope for from Russia is friendly neutrality and the
exercise of her powers of coercion.

Under these repeated blows the conspirator of Plombières began to see the gradual destruction of his dream. He
passed through one of those crises of anxious doubt in which
his will deserted him, his attention wandered, and his brain
refused to produce anything but contradictory, fugitive,
and confused thoughts. His disordered mind continually
vacillated between peace and war. The fears which were
weighing on him seemed to be written on his face; his
complexion was pale; his forehead wrinkled; his mouth
slack; his eye wandering and dull. By the 28 January—
that is to say, two days after he had signed the Treaty of

Alliance with Piedmont—his distress struck all those who approached him. Marshal de Castellane, whom he had sent for that day, writes in his diary: " The Emperor wore a sad, preoccupied air. I gathered from our conversation that, if the Emperor had an idea of making war, he now begins to feel the necessity of renouncing it." *Two days* after the signature of the alliance !

The English ambassador did not fail to observe this moral crisis, and to advise his chief at the Foreign Office, Lord Malmesbury. The latter was clever enough to see at once the advantage which might be gained. He proposed to the Emperor to send Lord Cowley to Vienna to try to open up official negotiations for a combined settlement of all Italian problems on the following principles : " Simultaneous withdrawal of the foreign troops occupying Bologna and Rome ; introduction of administrative reforms in the Italian States ; abrogation of the treaties which made the duchies of Parma and Modena fiefs of the Habsburg monarchy ; re-establishment of good relations between Austria and Piedmont." At the Tuileries this proposal was accepted with warm gratitude. In order to facilitate the mission of the British ambassador, Napoleon III even published in the *Moniteur* on 5 March an angry note in which he denied the warlike intentions which had been attributed to him : " these absurd rumours, invented by malice, which credulity spreads and stupidity accepts." He categorically declared that he had promised the King of Piedmont that he would defend him from Austrian oppression—and nothing more. Napoleon must have been entirely lacking in conscience to have made such assertions in the official organ of the

Empire, for had he not at Plombières plotted with Cavour the means of compelling Austria to take the offensive—not to mention the rest of their plans ?

The publication of this note immediately calmed the public mind ; everything began to recover ; prices of stocks on the Bourse rose briskly. The general optimism received a further impetus three days later when it was known that Prince Napoleon was leaving the Ministry of Algiers. No doubt was felt that his resignation covered a disgrace, and the approaching fall of Cavour began to be discussed.

As, however, the British Government was struggling to turn to account the conciliatory tendencies which Lord Cowley had discovered in negotiating with the Emperor Francis Joseph and Count Buol, Prince Gortchakoff solemnly made the unexpected proposal of a congress. The fact of his taking the initiative in this manner was singular, un-expected, and extremely unfortunate ; for it thwarted the wise manœuvre of the British Government and, under the pretext of giving a wider scope to the negotiations, called their whole existence in question. At that time no one under-stood who had suggested this idea to the Tsar's minister ; nowadays it is well known that it came from the Russian ambassador at Paris, General Kisseleff, to whom Napoleon III had secretly suggested it.

Congresses were always his obsession ; to preside at a sort of Areopagus or an œcumenical council was his devouring ambition. Hypnotised by the Age of the Antonines and the majesty of the " Roman peace," he believed himself called upon by Providence to renew this miracle of history by spreading over the whole world the august benefits of the

PRINCE METTERNICH.

" Napoleonic peace." Seven months previously, under the shades of Plombières, he had sought with Cavour to find a means by which to compel Austria to commit " one of those nice little aggressive acts " against Piedmont. At that time he imagined himself already repeating the exploits of Arcola and Marengo, leading his armies over the Alps up to the very gates of Vienna, for Austria would never yield " until the sword had been driven into her heart."

Behold him returning in memory to his famous Bordeaux speech : " The Empire is peace ! ... Glory belongs to it by right of inheritance, but not war. Woe to him who is the first to give the signal for a conflict in Europe ! " For this reason he blindly agreed to all the terms of the Russian proposal : that the five great Powers—France, England, Austria, Prussia, and Russia—should alone participate in the congress ; that the Italian Question should be settled without the assistance of Piedmont ; that, moreover, the principles of 1815 should be maintained ; and, finally, that before any deliberations took place the Cabinet of Turin should be ordered to cease its military preparations. Confronted with this sudden *volte-face*, Lord Cowley was justified in writing : " I do not know what the Emperor desires. I am incapable of disentangling the true from the false in what he says." The weak Emperor, however, had reckoned without Cavour.

VI

For many weeks Cavour had been observing anxiously the change that was taking place in his ambiguous ally : a change which was likely to lead to an open rupture of the Alliance. He knew that there was only one method of dealing with variable natures like that of Napoleon III—moral suasion supported by the irresistible logic of facts. He therefore openly hurried on his warlike preparations in order to make it understood at the Tuileries that the die was cast ; that the hour of subterfuges and diplomatic manœuvres had gone by ; and that, under no pretext whatever, would Piedmont suffer any retreat, concession, or delay. Each time the Emperor showed signs of giving way, Cavour redoubled his efforts. First, he promulgated a decree by which many classes of the reserve were called to the colours ; next, he openly organised a voluntary regiment of Lombard and Venetian rebels against Austria ; then, he allowed sensational revelations to appear in the Press concerning the approaching revolt of the whole Peninsula ; and, finally, by means of a letter from the King to Prince Napoleon, he let it be known that he feared that some chance incident might compel Piedmont to commence hostilities. When, however, a Congress was proposed, and when Napoleon III, in spite of his pledges, agreed to submit the Italian Question to the arbitrament of Europe and, as a preliminary to the discussion, to gag the mouth of Piedmont, Cavour hastened to Paris.

In arranging an immediate audience with the Emperor for Cavour, Prince Napoleon permitted himself an outburst of indignation with his cousin : " In the Crimean War the Piedmontese soldiers were thought worthy to fight side by side with those of the Great Powers. King Victor Emmanuel was honoured by being permitted to lavish the blood and treasure of his people on behalf of those same Great Powers who to-day, in a purely Italian question, show him the door. A decision of the utmost gravity is to be taken without his even being heard! Obviously, Sire, you have meditated the consequences of this deed. The renewal of the Holy Alliance! The doom of the Italian people! The tyranny of the strong over the weak! The abrogation of the treaty with Piedmont, and the betrayal of concerted plans and agreements! It means that you will lead an expedition from Rome against Piedmont; and that means an upheaval in Italy. I can see what will come of it, as clearly as I see the sun. Either M. de Cavour will resign and my father-in-law abdicate, explaining to the world their motives for so doing, or Piedmont will protest against the holding of a congress and, after an heroic resistance by force of arms, perish. A great people will then have been sacrificed and a great cause lost! If you have any illusions as to this, events will have destroyed them before eight days have passed." On 26 March, with nerves still quivering from the fury of this outburst, Napoleon III received Cavour.

For the first time since their meeting at Plombières the two men stood face to face. Not, indeed, on an equal footing, since the one was the autocratic sovereign of one of the greatest empires in the world and the other only the representative of a paltry kingdom to which the Great Powers would not even accord a hearing. But by reason of his vivid personality, the temper and magnetism of his will-power, his command of incisive and powerful arguments, the keenness of his glance resembling the flash of a sword, the lesser man was the stronger of the two.

The mystery that enshrouds their interview will never be solved. All that is known is that Cavour violently opposed the intention to submit the Italian Question—that is to say, the entire imprescriptible rights of a nation—to the arbitrary decision of a political synod; that he no less violently refused a reduction in the strength of the Piedmontese army as a condition preliminary to the assembling of a congress. One cannot doubt that he also threatened the Emperor with his resignation, if France abandoned Piedmont in the decisive hour, and—direr threat still—with his intention to go to the United States to publish there the proofs of their conspiracy. Was he still more audacious? Did he evoke before Napoleon III the ghost of Orsini? Here, however, one enters upon the region of hypothesis. At least it is not beyond the bounds of possibility that at moments during this serious interview the Emperor saw written upon the walls of his study, as at Balthazar's feast, the terrible words of the assassin: *So long as Italy is not free, the peace of Your Majesty and of Europe will be no more than a dream.* Whatever passed between them, Cavour's attack was certainly a violent one: the next day, and on the day following, the Emperor remained in bed.

In Court circles the Emperor's indisposition was quickly understood, and the Austrian ambassador at once noted it in his diary: " Perhaps through the agonies he is now enduring, through his knowledge of the dangers that surround him, *through the tortures which M. de Cavour is inflicting on him even as I write these lines*—perhaps the Emperor Napoleon is expiating his sin; perhaps he will renounce completely the error of his ways."

While the unhappy monarch sought to restore his strength by rest, Cavour had long interviews with Walewski, Lord

Cowley, General Kisseleff, Prince Napoleon, and the intimates of the Palais Royal. On 29 March he again saw the
Emperor, this time in the presence of the Minister for Foreign
Affairs. But he obtained from him only vague promises,
assurances of sympathy, and counsels of moderation. A want
of cordiality marked their parting. As he entered the
express for Milan, Cavour said to the large company which
had come to bid him farewell : " The Emperor parted from
me with a cunning look. I certainly do not wish him to
get the better of us." This sally was unworthy of his far-
sightedness : instead of cursing, he should have rejoiced.
If the tangible outcome of his visit had been little, the moral
results were great. He had regained his ascendancy over
the Emperor ; he had brought him back into the right road ;
he had finally closed all ways of retreat against him ; still
more, he had placed him in the terrifying dilemma—" war
or dishonour." It would be war.

The chancelleries of the Great Powers throughout the
weeks that followed strove might and main to bring about
that congress which was the final chance of peace ; they
only succeeded, however, in exchanging meaningless phrases,
barren formulas, for diplomatic expedients could not prevail
against the resistless force of facts. On 23 April, when the
limits of her patience had been reached, Austria despatched
by the hand of a special envoy, Baron Kellersberg, a summons
to Piedmont to effect a reduction in her armaments within
the space of three days. At six o'clock on the evening of
26 April, the Piedmontese Government rejected this ultimatum. After the Austrian envoy had taken his leave, Cavour
walked through the passage leading from his study amidst

an anxious crowd. With a face of joy, he exclaimed:
" *Alea jaƈta eſt !* The lot is caſt ! . . . We have made hiſtory.
Now let us go and dine ! "

The next day the Auſtrian army, under the command of
General Giulay, received orders from Vienna to cross the
frontier. Two days later Prince Schwartzenberg's army
crossed the Ticino at Pavia.

CHAPTER VII

SOLFERINO AND VILLAFRANCA

CHAPTER VII

SOLFERINO AND VILLAFRANCA

I

SINCE Victor Emmanuel had left to take over the supreme command of the army, which he retained until the arrival of the French, Cavour had remained alone in the capital, and had added to his duties as President of the Council and Minister for Foreign Affairs, the portfolios of the Interior, War, and the Navy. He also assumed control of the vital services for national defence. To cope with these onerous tasks he remained constantly at his place of work, never leaving his office and taking no more than five hours' sleep at night. The provisioning of the army, the national food supply, levies, stores, arsenals, forage, transport, were one and all matters for his direct and personal supervision. In this work he had full scope for the employment of his genius for administration, for his driving power, and for those qualities of improvisation and disposition which had formerly won for Louvois the titles of " great contractor " and " great victualler." Side by side with this overwhelming labour he carried on another task no less arduous and much more delicate : that of inciting the small Italian States against their hated rulers.

His plans for a rising were so well organised, and his collaborators, Pallavicino and La Farina, so astute and so assiduous, that on 27 April Florence dethroned her Grand Duke. Next, Massa, Carrara, Parma, Plaisance, and Modena overthrew their rulers. At the same moment insurrection burst forth in the Papal States, where Bologna, Ravenna, Forli, Fano, Sinigaglia, Ancona, and Prouse tore down the Papal arms and unfurled the national colours. As each State became free the inhabitants looked to Piedmont and besought the guidance of Victor Emmanuel.

But Cavour's first thought after unloosing revolution was to keep it within bounds, and he sent into these States proconsular representatives chosen for their wisdom and strength of character. To each he gave identical instructions : " Maintain order at all costs ; make superhuman efforts on behalf of the war ; after victory is won, it will be time enough to consider political problems ! " He was indeed anxious to install the House of Savoy in the greater part of the Peninsula before Napoleon III, rendered still more powerful through victory, should have the time and the means to oppose Piedmontese ambitions and carry out his own schemes. The sagacious Cavour is said to have repeated to himself each morning La Fontaine's fable of the Sheep, the Goat, and the Lion.

II

Since the rejection of the Austrian ultimatum Cavour was no longer enamoured of his powerful ally. As by a miracle, a sudden change had come over public opinion in France : the Italian war had aroused the innate enthusiasm of the French. Mérimée hastened to convey this good news to his friend Panizzi : " We are a strange people ! Fifteen days ago I wrote to you that not a man in France desired the war, and I am convinced that I wrote the truth. To-day the contrary is true. French feeling is awakened. An enthusiasm has been aroused that is at once magnificent and terrifying. The nation hails the war with joy, full of confidence and spirit. As for the troops, they go off as to a ball. As they marched through the streets on the way to the stations the people covered them with flowers, gave them wine, and embraced them with adjurations to kill as many Austrians as they could. Each soldier carried a bouquet on his rifle. In this French gaiety there lies concealed one of the elements of victory : our race believes itself incapable of defeat. The bankers and men of fashion deeply regret this deplorable enthusiasm; but the masses are for the war, and the Emperor is more popular than ever."

Stimulated at once by this unexpected revival of his personal popularity, forgetting the nightmare in which he had lately been plunged, filled with self-confidence, seeing his star once more in the ascendant, Napoleon III addressed a solemn proclamation to the nation in which he set forth the reasons that had led France to take up arms : " We go to deliver a people groaning under foreign tyranny. Austria has brought matters to such a pass that either she must rule as far as the Alps or Italy must be free as far as the Adriatic ! " On 12 May he disembarked in Genoa from the *Queen Hortense*. The sun blazed down with the brilliance of a hot summer's day. Against the sparkling background of sea and sky this town of marble palaces, rising tier upon tier on its amphitheatre of hills, was like an enchanted city. As the launch bearing Cæsar and the fate of Italy sped forth from the Imperial vessel, roses were showered upon it from the hundreds of small boats escorting it, as were it the galley of Cleopatra on the waters of Cydnus. The long quays were crowded with an immense multitude, a picturesque and multi-coloured throng. Suddenly a great shout rent the air, dominating the clamour of the bells and the thunder of the cannon. Never even in the heroic days of the great Doria had the ancient ducal city vibrated to a livelier emotion. On the landing-stage the Prince of Carignan and the President of the Council stood waiting to greet the Emperor in the name of the King. The salutations at an end, the procession set out for the Palazzo Reale, the centre of delirious acclamation and moving under triumphal arches, streamers, and flowers.

Astounded and fascinated, his eyes flashing, his cheeks pale, Napoleon III felt all the memories and dreams of the past surge through his mind. Suddenly he noticed Cavour, who was seated facing him, and said, to him solemnly : " It is a quarter of a century since my brother died in my arms on behalf of Italy and since my mother snatched me from Austria's talons ! " The pageant continued until the evening with receptions, a great banquet, and a performance at the Opera. As a conclusion to this day of apotheosis and intoxication the Emperor announced to his troops that he had assumed the command :

" Soldiers !

" I have come to place myself at your head and to lead you into battle. We march to the help of a nation demanding its independence and seeking to overthrow an alien tyranny. . . . . There is no need for me to excite your ardour : each step will remind you of a victory. Along the Sacred Way of ancient Rome inscriptions upon marble stood to remind the people of their great deeds. To-day you will march along another Sacred Way through Mondovi, Marengo, Lodi, Castiglione, Arcola, Rivoli, of glorious memory. France expects great things of you. To-day, throughout the length and breadth of France, resound these words of happy augury : the new army of Italy will be worthy of the old ! "

Two days later Napoleon III arrived at his headquarters at Alessandria. Great strategical operations were about to begin, for the adversaries were already at grips. On the one side 120,000 French and 56,000 Piedmontese ; on the other, 132,000 Austrians. Up to this time the Emperor had never conducted a war : he was fifty-one, or five years older than his uncle on the day of Waterloo. Moreover, these five additional years coincided with a period in his life in which his passions had visibly fatigued him. By chance, he had as opponent the most timid and hesitating of gene-ralissimos—the artillery General Count Giulay. After many gropings and miscalculations, orders and counter-orders, marches and counter-marches, the Allies developed an offensive on a wide front in the district of the Upper Ticino between Novara and Turbigo. Victors at Magenta on 4 June, they entered Milan three days later.

This fortunate opening to the campaign exceeded Cavour's fondest hopes ; but it was only the opening. Retiring in good order on the Mincio, the Austrian army lost no oppor-tunity of taking the offensive. Reinforcements were con-tinuously arriving by way of the Semmering, and the army would shortly attain the famous quadrilateral of Verona, where it could be reorganised at leisure. Finally, the *moral* of the troops was excellent, especially since the incapable Giulay had resigned his command and had been succeeded by the young Emperor Francis Joseph in person. Taking these circumstances into account, the war would probably be long and bitter. Cavour was unable to forget that the Emperor had said to him at Plombières that a great effort would be necessary on the part of the Allies in order to expel the Habsburgs from the Peninsula : " There is no use in concealing the fact. Austria has immense military resources ; the campaigns of the First Empire proved that only too well. Two or three battles lost in the valleys of the Po and the Tagliamento will not be sufficient to induce her to renounce Italy. We shall have to besiege the fortresses of the Quadrilateral ; to hold the highways of Tyrol ; and to march on Vienna through Carinthia. We shall need at least three hundred thousand men ! "

The order of the day addressed by the Emperor to the army from Genoa shows that he persisted in this opinion. For the Sacred Way along which Bonaparte had left indelible marks on the map of history, did not stop at the Cisalpine plains ; it passed over the hill of Tarvis and came to Campo-Formio by Leoben.

Never losing sight of this ulterior phase of the war, Cavour worked unceasingly to provoke a Magyar insurrection. He invited Kossuth and Klapka to Turin ; he secretly sent 20,000 rifles to the national committees at Budapest by way of Galatz and the Danube ; he formed a legion of Hungarian volunteers in the Piedmontese army.

On 24 June the Allies won the battle of Solferino. That night Napoleon III telegraphed to the Empress : " *A great battle and a great victory !* " But in truth it was a desultory, disorganised, and scattered battle—a " soldier's battle," as it has been styled in order to denote the want of any supreme or guiding direction. In short, one of those tumultuous hecatombs, confused and unbelievable, which in Tolstoy's eyes were a summary of all the skill of great military leaders. A sterile victory in that, in the intoxication of his triumph, Napoleon III neglected to order any pursuit, although his cavalry had been engaged hardly at all. Hence the Austrians retired without discomfiture behind the barrier of the Adige and under the protection of the guns of Verona. During their easy retirement the French army remained stationary. On 6 July, twelve days after the battle, it was still encamped on the banks of the Mincio, only 10 kilometres from Solferino.

This amazing inaction did not fail to astonish and, above all, to disquiet Cavour. Since 1 July he had scented " some diplomatic plot to stop the victorious march of the Allies at the Adige, if not at the Mincio." He took the greatest pains to keep himself informed of the state of affairs. For many reasons his relations with the supreme command were very strained : the inevitable quarrel between civilian and soldier in time of war. La Marmora and Della Rocca— the chiefs of the Headquarters Staff—sought to confine him to his administrative functions, and whenever he questioned them on the plan of campaign they did not hesitate to reply : " He who pays the piper calls the tune." The King treated him with as scant courtesy. Happy at last in the life which

pleased him best—that warrior's life of fatigue, peril, and
glory which Henri IV called " the true food of the really
royal mind "—Victor Emmanuel shook off the heavy tutelage
of his minister and displayed a wicked delight in beholding
him quarrelling with his officers. With them the King
always sided.

On 8 July Cavour learned by a devious way that General
Fleury, aide-de-camp-in-chief to the Emperor, had gone to
Verona to propose an armistice to Francis Joseph. The
following evening a telegram brought him the news that
the armistice had been concluded. When this news reached
him his faithful secretary, Nigra, was with him. Cavour said
to him : " What do you think of this ? " The youthful
diplomat was too well acquainted with his chief's preoccupa-
tions to hesitate for a moment : " It means peace," he said.
" Then let us go at once. We can still be in time."

On the morning of 10 July the railway deposited them
at Desenzano on the shores of Lake Garda, where the war
zone began. Thence a peasant's wagon brought them in
two hours to the Piedmontese Headquarters at Monzambano
on the Mincio. Cavour at once hurried to the King, who
was living in the suburbs in the Villa Melchiorri. No sooner
was he alone with the King, and the doors closed behind
them, than their loud voices penetrated beyond the walls
of the house. What took place in that little drawing-room
of a provincial villa was indeed as dramatic as a scene from
Shakespeare.

Victor Emmanuel was forced to admit at the very beginning that on the eve of Solferino—that is to say, *eighteen
days before*—Napoleon III had confided to him that he was

resolved soon to treat with the Austrians on account of the. threatening attitude of the German States ; and the King had assented, saying that, after all, this abbreviated war would at least bring him Lombardy. Was it not the only reasonable course possible ? If France gave up the fight, would Piedmont be strong enough to carry it on alone ? Moreover, not very long before this, the Emperor had solemnly averred that the armistice was simply a military truce and would not in any way prejudice the terms of peace. He had even added : " Be assured that I will impose very hard conditions—very hard ! " At each of these phrases Cavour started under the increasing fury of his anger. The thought of all he could have done ; of all the schemes he would have been able to devise ; of all the resources he could have brought into play during those *eighteen days* if he had been at once told of Napoleon III's intentions— this it was that filled him with fury. The feeble arguments advanced by the King still further enraged him, and he tore them to shreds. Negotiations with Austria before she had been driven from the Peninsula meant the end of the *Risorgi-mento* ; the ruin of the national hopes ; the useless sacrifice of the thousands of Italians who had fallen on the field of battle ; the repudiation of the leadership assumed by Pied-mont in Italy ; the disgrace, the unpardonable disgrace, of the House of Savoy ! Since Napoleon had resolved to negotiate with the enemy in the full tide of war it remained only for Piedmont to forsake the offender and carry on the combat alone. " If we perish, at least it shall be with heads unbowed ! " In vain Victor Emmanuel tried to overcome Cavour—to make him see reason. Was it not wiser to stop the war when Lombardy had been won rather than break with the French at the risk of returning to Turin empty-handed, and pursued by Austrian bayonets amidst the laughter of Europe? Cavour, no longer able to contain himself, cried out: "Then, Sire, abdicate!" "Be silent! Remember that I am the King!" "No, at this moment I am the true king!" "You the King? You are nothing but an impudent fellow!" Shaking with rage, Victor Emmanuel quitted the scene, slamming the door violently behind him.

Without an instant's delay Cavour betook himself to the French Headquarters in the town of Valeggio about five kilometres from Monzambano. By exerting great pressure on Napoleon III, might it not be possible to avert the catastrophe? But the Sphinx was invisible, meditating a dramatic stroke for the morrow. Enraged, off went Cavour to see Prince Napoleon, expecting to be received with open arms by him at any rate. Alas! what a disillusionment! Victor Emmanuel's son-in-law, having first done all in his power to provoke the war, to-day was as eager, violent, acrimonious, and sharp in his advocacy of the immediate conclusion of peace. Why this sudden desertion of the Italian cause, this blustering apostasy? Because a mission that had occasioned his visiting Florence, and all that he had very accurately observed during the past two months, had revealed to him that his beautiful kingdom of Tuscany had no more substantiality than a castle in the air: all Central Italy was in the possession of Piedmont. Thus, feeling duped and mystified, he was as irritated as if he had received a personal injury. Instead of compassionating Cavour's agonies, he snubbed him well. " Of course we must make peace, and at once. Otherwise we shall be attacked on the Rhine, and then you will not come to our aid." Cavour recalled the solemn promises of Napoleon III : " Italy free even to the Adriatic." " Any peace that does not free Venice will be a betrayal. When one has taken such engagements before the whole world, one must fulfil them ! " But the Prince was not the man to be nonplussed : " Do you really think that we would lose France and our dynasty for you ? " " Then," Cavour retorted, " we will carry on the war by ourselves ; we will let loose revolution throughout the Peninsula ; we will raise armies of volunteers." " Ah ! I know your volunteers. I have seen them in Florence. They told me there were thirty thousand. Do you know how many actually came ? Four thousand ! And what a collection ! A race of degenerates, corrupt, contemptible, unfit for liberty, unworthy of all the sacrifices that have been made for them ! " Carried away by his virulent fury, the Prince was inexhaustible in pouring contumely on the degeneracy of the Italians. At last Cavour, fuming and suffocating with rage, succeeded in stemming the torrent of invective. " I know, I know. . . . Give your dog a bad name, and hang him ! " After this mortifying scolding, Cavour returned to Monzambano conscious of the approach of an inevitable and imminent catastrophe.

III

Fascinated by the great Napoleonic legend, Napoleon III desired to inscribe in the annals of his reign an interview at Tilsit. For the following day, 11 July, he had

15

therefore arranged a meeting with Francis Joseph at Villafranca.

But Tilsit had been staged in order to announce to the world the commencement of a new order of things and—as Bossuet would have phrased it—" the opening of a new epoch in the progress of time." Villafranca, however, was merely a still-life deception; it served to conceal a retreat, the shattering of an illusion, and the miscarriage of an ill-conceived enterprise.

Since his triumphal arrival at Genoa and those brilliant days when he had invited his troops to follow the Sacred Way, Cæsar Imperator had, as it were, shed a fragment of his dream at each step. Authoritative testimony exists concerning this personal drama: the letters and notes of his aide-de-camp-in-chief, General Fleury.

First had come the military discomfitures. The Emperor had been quick to perceive that he could not suddenly make a commander-in-chief of himself at the age of fifty-one. " War," declared the prisoner at St. Helena, " is a simple art consisting entirely in achievements." But Napoleon III did not possess a single one of the natural aptitudes essential to the practice of this art. Wanting in a sense of topography, his reading of maps ended in confusion. The vague and abstract nature of his thoughts did not make him less incapable of leading an army. Division of forces, planning of marches and organising of supplies, manœuvres, choice of ground, tactical problems, the question of reserves, the movements of the enemy, etc., floated before his mental vision in a disorderly and nebulous fashion. Never once did he have a clear, real, swift, and sharp apprehension of a situation ; never once one of those concise and luminous intuitions which reveal as by a lightning-flash a whole group of facts in all their relations, their ordering, and their immediate or eventual results. Hence there was to be found in his military orders so much of incoherence and confusion that when the campaign was over he had the records of his Headquarters Staff burnt in order to avoid the judgment of History. General Fleury shows clearly that " the material difficulties of the war wearied the Emperor and caused him by degrees to reconsider his idea of commanding a great army." At Magenta, too, Napoleon III had known mortal fear. For three hours he had stood immovable on the bridge of San Martino, all his reserves exhausted, looking on with horror at the frightful slaughter, ignorant of the whereabouts of his commanders, understanding nothing of the progress of the battle, never giving an order, alarming his Staff by his wild eyes and listless manner, remaining in a kind of moral collapse until the instant when from the direction of Buffalora there came the roar of MacMahon's rescuing cannon. During these tragic hours he had seen the destruction of his army, the ruin of his fortune ; he had sounded the depths of the abyss. Next day Fleury wrote to his wife : " It's a victory, to be sure. But what tears, what blood ! If it were to begin again, I feel sure the Emperor could not stand it." A few days later he again wrote : " If we had lost the bridge over the canal, we should have been driven back into the Ticino. God knows what would then have happened to the Emperor and to France ! "

After Solferino, the Emperor's humane heart had not

been able to bear the sight of all the dead and writhing bodies, of all the wounded that strewed the battle-field. More than thirty thousand ! " War is magnificent from a distance," Fleury had written. " It benefits the commanders-in-chief, and glorifies countries ; but it costs many tears." Gazing on the bodies of his soldiers, the Emperor had been tormented by the thought that " so many brave men have laid down their lives for a people who do not love them and for a cause whose future is veiled in doubt." And Fleury had continued to write that " these butcheries do not belong to our age. One finds it difficult to regard the Austrians as enemies and still more difficult to think of this degenerate people whom we have come to deliver from bondage, as friends. The welfare of Italy, who does not wish to be happy, is not worth the bloody sacrifice imposed upon our army."

The indecisive victory of Solferino had posed a difficult problem for Napoleon III to solve. He had stood before the great fortresses of the Quadrilateral. To attack or besiege them would have required 300,000 men, and he had had at the most 100,000.

But the disillusionments and problems which he had experienced as generalissimo were nothing to those created for him by the diplomatic situation in Europe. Before Napoleon III had even left Paris, Walewski had predicted that the war could not long be localised and that Germany would seek to attack him on the Rhine while he was engaged on the Adige. It had then seemed that this prediction was about to be fulfilled. Since Magenta, Germany had been in a state of effervescence and all parts of the country flamed with warlike ardour. Before long Prussia had placed herself at the head of the movement, and at her request the Federal Diet had ordered the mobilisation of 350,000 men. While this army was concentrating in the Rhenish provinces, a summons was to be addressed to Napoleon III to evacuate Lombardy, and in the event of his refusal France was to be invaded. In the path of the invaders there had stood an army of 60,000 men, nearly all of whom were conscripts : in other words, the road to Paris had lain open before them.

On receipt of this alarming news the Emperor had looked to Russia for help, invoking the celebrated agreements of Warsaw and Stuttgart. Once again Walewski had been proved to be in the right, for these so-called agreements were purely verbal—*verba et voces, prætereaqua nihil.* Then, too, the sentiments of the Tsar had recently undergone a change. When he had seen Austria a little humiliated and beaten, as he had wished to see her, he was quite satisfied. On the other hand, he had no desire to see the uprising of revolutionary ideas in Italy and, above all, the insolent triumph of that new idea—the principle of nationality— which was so hateful to him in Poland. He was firmly attached to the House of Hohenzollern by family traditions and for reasons of State. Thus, while he exercised a gentle influence in Berlin in order to allay the fury of Germany, he had addressed this pressing advice to the victor of Solferino : " Be quick to make peace ; otherwise you will be attacked on the Rhine."

Finding himself in this cruel dilemma, Napoleon III endeavoured to persuade the British Government to mediate between the belligerents. But the British Cabinet had deemed it wise to leave him to extricate himself from the troubles his mad adventure had brought him. At this juncture the idea had come to him to send his clever aide-de-camp, General Fleury, to Verona to request an interview with Francis Joseph.

The interview was fixed for 11 July at nine o'clock in the morning in the village of Villafranca, situated half-way between Verona and Valeggio. Chivalrous by nature, Napoleon III arrived first at the rendezvous and went about a quarter of a league to meet his youthful enemy, as though to make the descendant of Maria Theresa and Charles V forget the defeats that had been inflicted upon him. The two monarchs entered a humble house—Casa Morelli. Their conference lasted barely an hour. Neither paper nor maps lay upon the table, for these were not two diplomats come to make a bargain : they were sovereigns desiring to settle a quarrel between their peoples. The Emperor of the French opened the conversation gallantly. " Sire, we can negotiate without loss of honour. Your troops and mine have fought with equal valour." The Austrian Emperor answered : " Like you, Sire, I desire peace. The arbitrament of war has pronounced against me, and I submit. In order to show Your Majesty the confidence with which you inspire me, I will indicate to you wholly and frankly the limits of the concessions I am prepared to make. I have lost Lombardy. I am ready to renounce it. But for reasons that you will be able to understand, I cannot cede it to Piedmont : I cede it to France, who can then dispose of it as she desires. I certainly wish to keep the fortresses of Peschiera and Mantua, since these are still in my possession."

Further, he agreed that the duchy of Parma should be transferred to the House of Savoy, while at the same time he
insisted that the rulers of Modena and Tuscany should be
re-established on their thrones. He promised to grant a
general amnesty for those of his subjects, Venetians and
Hungarians, who had rendered themselves liable to loss. of
civil rights through participation in the war. On these
bases Napoleon III expressed his readiness to negotiate. He
demanded in return that Venetia should be united to a
confederation of Italian States over which the Pope would
hold the honorary presidency. "Your Majesty will then
find yourself," Napoleon III observed to Francis Joseph,
"in regard to this province in an analogous position to that
of the King of Holland, who, as ruler of Luxembourg,
is a member of the German Confederation." With an air
of indifference Francis Joseph assented to this bizarre and
unexpected request that would give Austria that right to
interfere in the domestic concerns of the Peninsula which
she had never explicitly obtained even in 1815. Finding
themselves thus in agreement, the two monarchs took
leave of one another with a handshake.

Napoleon III returned to Valeggio with his mind freed
from a great anxiety. Philip de Commines said of the
Constable de Saint-Pol, who had drifted unresisting to
his fate : "I have known in my life few people who knew
how to run away in time." The malicious counsellor of
Louis XI would have greatly approved of the "flight" of
Villafranca. But it was just in time!

In the course of the day Prince Napoleon went to Verona
to submit to Francis Joseph the formal draft of the pre-

liminaries agreed upon in the morning. After a short discussion the Emperor signed the document, saying with a sigh : " I am making a great sacrifice in ceding my most beautiful province."

As Victor Emmanuel saw it, the " sacrifice " was too small. When he learned from Napoleon the terms of peace—those terms about which his ally had never even consulted him—he exclaimed : " Unhappy Italy ! . . . What is this ? Not only have we not gained Venetia, but we are refused Peschiera, Mantua, and Modena ! And Austria will continue to domineer over the Peninsula ! What a disaster ! What a downfall ! " His shaking left hand plucked at the sword-knot of his sabre. Before long, conscious of the dignity required of his royal position, he recovered himself ; nor did he forget to recall the debt he nevertheless owed to France. " Despite my regrets, I assure Your Majesty that I will never forget what you have accomplished for the Italian cause, and I entreat you to believe I will always be your loyal friend."

About eleven o'clock that night the King retraced his steps to Monzambano with a heart full of bitterness. It was a thundery night of stifling heat. Arrived in his study, he began by divesting himself of his sabre, his cravat, his collar, and his tunic ; he unbuttoned his shirt and exposed his great hairy chest to the air ; then, in this state of disattire which was customary with him, he summoned Cavour and La Marmora. " Read ! " he said to the minister, in handing him a copy of the fatal convention. With a lightning-like glance Cavour had read everything and understood everything. " Your Majesty, you will not sign this ; it is too ignominious ! . . . We are given Lombardy—and to what purpose when the rest of the Peninsula remains under Habsburg tyranny ? You have not the right to place the signature of Piedmont at the foot of a treaty that not only does not free Venetia but that legalises and confirms the hegemony of Austria in Modena, Bologna, Florence, Rome, and throughout the whole of Italy. No, no, you will not sign that ! Your duty is beyond question : even without the support of France you must carry on the war. If you are beaten— well ! you will abdicate." Brusquely the King interrupted him : " That will do ! I will not have your insolence of yesterday repeated." " Then I ask Your Majesty to accept my resignation." " I accept it. You have leave to retire."

Alone with La Marmora, Victor Emmanuel gave vent to his anger. " Since he wishes to go, let him go ! I am at least rid of his arrogance and tyranny. . . . Besides, he has lost his head ; he needs rest."

On 13 July Cavour returned to Turin to take charge of affairs until the appointment of his successor. The many friends who had come to welcome him at the railway-station were alarmed at his appearance : in three days he had aged years. That morning the news of the Treaty of Villafranca had plunged the capital into a sort of stupor, as on the night of Novara. Every face was frightened, grief-stricken, or sinister. Here and there groups were gathered, exclaiming with menacing gestures : " Napoleon has again betrayed us ! Impostor and perjurer in 1849 ; impostor and perjurer in 1859 ; for ever impostor and perjurer ! The murderer of the Roman Republic has set a noble crown upon his villainous work. He has only pretended to wish to free

Italy that he may the better plunge his dagger into her. Ah! when will our day of vengeance dawn?" Suddenly, as by order or as though waved there by a magic wand, the portrait of Orsini appeared on the front of all the buildings and shops.

That same day Napoleon III, anxious to return to France, or rather, to quit Italian soil, handed over the command of his army. He avoided Genoa because in this impetuous city his stirring apotheosis of 12 May would have taken on another character. Instead, he went directly to Turin and left on the following day, very early in the morning, for Mont Cenis. Victor Emmanuel dutifully accompanied him, less from courtesy than from a desire to shield him, if necessary, under his cloak of authority. Nor was the precaution unnecessary. The citizens of Turin, customarily so placid, were so enraged that the police deemed it wise to add a regiment of French cavalry to the Royal escort.

After greeting the two monarchs as they descended from their train, Cavour took his leave, and refused to appear at the farewell banquet which the King had been unable to avoid giving for his guest. But in the evening he was summoned to the palace. The Emperor wished to speak to him for a few minutes. "I did not receive you at Valeggio because I had made up my mind, irrevocably made up my mind, to make peace. What could I do? To continue the war would require three hundred thousand men; I have not them." Cavour refrained from arguing with him, and contented himself with making a few reflections on the sad fate of the Italian provinces once more fallen under the yoke of their former masters. "Have no fear," Napoleon III assured him, " I will plead their cause before the approaching Congress. . . . I will also repeat to you what I have already said to the King : that since Piedmont has not secured all that was promised her by our alliance, I renounce the annexation of Nice and Savoy." For the laſt time the conspirators of Plombières ſtood face to face. The chains with which they had bound themselves and each other juſt a year ago compelled them to work again, either the one with the other or the one againſt the other ; but they did not respeſt each other.

On 17 July the Emperor reached Saint-Cloud. The newspapers and reports which he had received during his journey had informed him that the preliminaries of Villa-franca had aroused a lively discontent in France. After the resounding proclamation of 3 May : " Italy muſt be free up to the Adriatic " ; after the official dithyrambs on the viſtories of Magenta and Solferino, the nation did not expeſt to see their army halted on the bank of the Mincio, Venice retained under the Habsburg sceptre, and the Auſtrian hegemony confirmed and legalised throughout the Peninsula. Un-willing to expose himself to a possible manifeſtation of ill-will on the part of the Parisians, Napoleon III gave orders that his train should be switched at Bercy on to the direſt line to Saint-Cloud. After a short reſt he assembled the legislative bodies to juſtify to them his premature conclusion of peace. " When after a glorious two months' campaign the Allied armies arrived beneath the walls of Verona, the nature of the war inevitably changed both in a military and a political sense. Fate compelled me to attack an enemy entrenched behind ſtrong fortresses. At the commencement of a long and sterile siege-warfare I found myself faced with a Europe that had taken up arms either to dispute our victory or to intensify our defeat. It became necessary to accept battle on the Rhine as well as on the Adige; to spill precious blood of which there was not a drop too much. . . . On behalf of the independence of Italy I went to war against the will of Europe; but since the destinies of France are imperilled, I have concluded peace." The confession was frank; the apology did not fail in either courage or spirit. But General Fleury was not wrong in interpolating this commentary in his diary: "Now, people will say, why did he make war if it involved the risk of raising Europe against him and of having to halt in the full tide of victory before the imminent danger of an invasion? It was brave, of course, on the Emperor's part to act as the saviour of Italy. But, if he knew this on the morrow of Solferino, he should have known it before setting out upon this crusade."

IV

Not without difficulty Victor Emmanuel had at last found another President of the Council, General La Marmora, a judicious man with a loyal and a resolute heart. He surrounded himself with energetic collaborators like Dabormida at the Ministry for Foreign Affairs, and Rattazzi at that of the Interior. Freed at last from all cares of office, Cavour left for Switzerland to stay with his loved cousins de La Rive at Pressinge, near Geneva. Two motives decided him to go: an imperative need for rest after three years of Herculean labour; and the desire to facilitate the work of the new ministers by sparing them the embarrassment of his presence and by loyally effacing himself.

Fall from power is the supreme moral test of statesmen. History is full of varied examples, from the calm and noble exile of Choiseul at Chantaloup to the vindicative, peevish, degrading retirement of Bismarck at Varsin. Cavour's example is not less worthy of being recorded, in that it did him honour, and heightened a predominant trait in his personality.

When he arrived at Pressinge his nerves were still on edge, his mind fevered, and his brain restless and excited. The early days of relaxation and idleness were cruel days for him. But the understanding affection of his cousins and the clever and discrete solicitude with which they surrounded him, enabled him to give himself up to his own thoughts freely. Although obviously exhausted physically, he was not by any means depressed, showing himself by turns sombre, agitated, detached, alert, talkative, silent, dreamy, sarcastic, and enflamed. It was clear that he unceasingly pondered upon his broken schemes, his frustrated designs, his ruined hopes. He frequently spoke of Napoleon III, and always in an ironical tone. " This unhappy Emperor did what he could at Villafranca. He is reproached for having renounced Venetia, the Romagna, Tuscany, Modena, Mantua, Peschiera. . . . He would certainly have granted more if Francis Joseph had been more insistent; he would have ceded Milan and Turin. . . . What could he do? He was tired; he was bored; he was hot."

Less than a month after his arrival, however, Cavour became suddenly transformed. He made an end of useless

recrimination and regret. Breathing the superb air of the
Alps, his powerful constitution healed itself, his buoyant
spirit rebounded. " It is not to the past that one must
look," he exclaimed one day ; " it is to the future. . . . I
followed one path. It was closed to me. Well! I will
follow another. We will take twenty years to achieve
what could have been done in some months. What else
can we do ? After all, England has done nothing for Italy
as yet. Every dog has his day, however! Now I will
occupy myself with Naples. They accuse me of being a
revolutionary—so much the worse for them! The first
thing to do is to go ahead, so we will go ahead ! " In this
alert and resolute mood he returned to Piedmont towards
the end of August and shut himself up at Léri.

There, while applying himself to everything with the
same spirit which he had formerly lavished upon the development of his country property, he meditated unceasingly
upon the consequences of the calamitous peace that he had
been unable to prevent. Numerous friends came to consult
and to visit him. To one and all he declared : " The Treaty
of Villafranca is not only criminal : it is absurd and inexcus-
able, and will be found incapable of execution. . . . The Italian
Question cannot be solved but by the independence and
unification of the whole Peninsula."

The chaotic events that took place in Central Italy during
the last months of this year, 1859, daily justified his prescience.
He did not content himself with abstract prophecies. An
idea never remained speculative and algebraic in his mind ;
his realistic temperament at once reduced it to concrete
terms. With an amazing agility he conceived even to the

moſt minute details an entirely new programme, an entirely
new policy, that would be able to make good the cataſtrophe
of Villafranca. But such was the audacity of this programme and policy that he alone was capable of carrying
them out. The great actor in the Italian drama had not yet
spoken his laſt word.

CHAPTER VIII

THE STATESMAN AND THE *CONDOTTIERE*

CHAPTER VIII

THE STATESMAN AND THE *CONDOTTIERE*

I

ON 20 January 1860 Cavour was recalled to the government. Recalled by force of circumstances, by the stern logic of facts. During the six months of his retirement his enemies, delighted at having at last escaped his despotic rule, plotted wildly against him. He knew the bitter fruits of unpopularity.

But a day came when even his worst detractors realised that he alone had the genius and the power necessary to resolve the insoluble problems of the moment. They were obliged to recognise that in resigning the ministry after Villafranca, he had not been influenced purely by ill-humour (as so many had thought), but that once again he had been inspired by a shrewd and prudent instinct. His violent abjuration of the disastrous peace identified him with the national conscience; in the minds of all Italians he abode as the resolute champion of a consecrated cause, the essential achiever of future revenge.

His weak successors, bending under their burden, petitioned Victor Emmanuel to ease them of the load and to place it again on Cavour's shoulders. The royal consent was not obtained without trouble, for the violent scenes at Monzambano were impressed on the King's memory. The idea of being once more subject to the pleasure of a collaborator

so imperious did not please him at all.   More than probably,
he thought, his contemptuous minister would only begin
to lecture him again on the enduring scandal of his amorous
life : then he would consent to Cavour's recall only if he
would take an oath never in the slightest degree to interfere
in his sovereign's intercourse with the beautiful Rosine.
Hardly was Cavour at the helm once more and a single turn
given to the wheel, when the ship of state came steadily
round again to her proper course.

As early as 25 January Cavour wrote to Prince Napoleon :
" The King's grace has recalled me to direct the affairs of
my country, and I feel the need of invoking, as in the past,
the favour and the protection of your Imperial Highness.
The sentiments of Your Highness towards Italy are always
the same, I know, and it is this fact that causes me to hope
that the sentiments with which Your Highness honoured me
for so long, remain unaltered too. . . . What changes since
my last interview with Your Highness ! How marvellously the
germs contained in the Treaty of Villafranca have developed !
The diplomatic campaign that followed it was as glorious
for the Emperor as, and more advantageous for Italy than,
the military campaign that preceded it. How often in my
solitude I cried : ' Blesséd be the Peace of Villafranca ! ' "
These words, almost stupefying from the pen of Cavour,
enable us to lay the finger on one of the most remarkable
traits of his political genius : the faculty of retracing his
steps.   After having heaped maledictions on the peace of
Villafranca, behold him lauding it to the skies ! The fact
was that even in its imperfections, in all that it contained of
the fanciful and the absurd, he had detected an unhoped-for

means of reattempting the national resurrection, and on a much larger scale, with vastly enlarged prospects of success. Following the course of events in the character of a mere looker-on, he had been much struck by the contradictions, the defeats, and finally the confusion, of the Napoleonic policy.

The preliminaries of Villafranca, sanctioned by the Treaty of Zurich, had satisfied none in France. The Liberals could see nothing in them but the maintenance of Austrian hegemony in the Peninsula. Prince Napoleon, his rôle at Valeggio already forgotten, did not hesitate to throw all the odium of the peace upon his imperial cousin; he would not set foot in Saint-Cloud again; he refused to participate in the ceremonies organised to welcome home the troops; he went as far as to say that the Emperor was a man of no capacity, that all Europe would henceforth recognise him as such, that he inspired confidence in none because all knew now that he did not speak the truth. The little court at the Palais Royal improved upon this tattle of course, declaring that " France could not survive with a constitution that placed power so excessive in one man's hands." The bourgeoisie, until then much attached to the Imperial House, were not less dissatisfied. " This war was folly! The Emperor was warned of the dangers he ran; but he would listen to nothing. It is too much of a good thing for him to come to us after two months of bloody fighting and say quite simply that he was mistaken! " The Catholic party were irritated to an extreme. " What's this? The Emperor, after guaranteeing the Pope the integrity of his States, left him and kidnapped the Romagna, the Marches, Umbria!

. . . And when will it be the Eternal City's turn ? " A chorus of violent protest rose from all the bishoprics. Thus was born, or rather was revived, the intricate " Roman Question," the question that carried so much weight in the destinies of the Second Empire that, without it, Sadowa, Sedan, would be inexplicable.

The position of Napoleon III with foreign Powers was more difficult than ever.

England—whose government was no longer in the hands of the Tory Lords Derby and Malmesbury, but in those of the Whig Lords Palmerston and John Russell—had unceremoniously changed her attitude towards Italy after Solferino. Until then very favourable to Austria, she had since warmly supported the most daring aspirations of Italian nationalism. Her aim clearly was to alienate from Napoleon III the sympathies of a people he had been ingenuous enough to liberate. She even soon conceived the idea of setting up in the Peninsula a strong, homogeneous, centralised State of which she would be the natural ally against French dominion. By this clever auction-room policy of outbidding, too, she would be able to stimulate in every possible way, the abhorrence in which the Italians held the transactions at Villafranca. According to Palmerston, England would not admit " the thraldom of Italy to be the final scene of a drama that had as prologue the declaration, ' Italy should be free as far as the Adriatic.' "

Prussia confronted the Cabinet of the Tuileries with stifled animosity, for Germanic passions were once again inflamed against France. Moreover, as early as October of this year, 1859—three months after Solferino—the Pied-

montese minister at Berlin had maintained to Baron von
Schleinitz, head of the Prussian Government, " that Germany
should aid the Italians to throw off the French yoke
and to set up a large, independent kingdom that, later,
could be of use to Germany in the furtherance of her
national ambitions. . . ." These words had fallen on
attentive ears.

The Tsar of Russia, Alexander II, considered that the
revolutionary notions of Napoleon III had lasted long enough :
" If he is not stopped, he will turn Europe topsy-turvy."
Gortchakoff was frank with Montebello : " A word in your
ear : Europe needs peace. If you continue to trouble her
periodically, you will never inspire confidence in anyone
again, and you will alienate your best friends." Without
waiting to see the effect of this warning, the Romanoff
monarchy drew closer the bonds of its friendship with
Prussia, and became again reconciled to Austria. From this
time on, an astute observer could see forming in the European
heavens that constellation that in 1870 left France completely
isolated in Germany's path.

The hub of all these complicated difficulties, the unhappy
Napoleon III, did not know what to do. Over every item
of his programme he hesitated, he shuffled, he put off, he
avoided, he contradicted himself. Thus the ruling idea,
the framework, of the edifice planned at Villafranca, the
Italian Confederation, he exhausted himself in vain to realise.
To introduce Austria into the federal organisation of the
Italian people, when she was already installed in Venice and
in redoubtable positions in the Quadrilateral was, according
to Palmerston, " to deliver up the Peninsula, tied hand and

foot, to her," or, according to d'Azeglio, "to set the fox
to keep the geese." As for the Presidency of the Confederation, the Pope spurned it vigorously; for it had as a corollary
the concession of a lay administration in the Romagna. The
Emperor lavished his best style on the Sovereign Pontiff
in an attempt to make his strange proposal agreeable: "It
is of grave consequence even to the honour of the Faith that
Your Holiness should preside over the destinies of Italy,
like the Doge of Venice, who by a gesture appeared to be
able to raise or to appease the billows of the Adriatic."
This noble metaphor drew a thin smile from Pius IX.
"Pretty, very pretty," he exclaimed; "the Doge raising
or appeasing by a gesture the billows of the Adriatic; . . .
but I will have none of his Confederation or of his lay
officials." Nothing could make him retract this *non pos-
sumus*. The enemies of the Holy See were naturally still more
hostile to this bizarre compound. "What," they said,
"the head, the guide, the inspirer of the new Italy to be
pontifical rule, a miserable rule, feeble, out of date, grown
old in routine and reaction, closed against every outside
influence—incapable of understanding the needs and the
tendencies of modern society! What an anachronism!
What absurdity!" English statesmen and journalists made
this argument one of their pet themes. Lord Malmesbury
wrote : "The whole world mocks at this peace and especially
at the ridiculous title of ' Honorary President of the Confederation' bestowed upon Pius IX. This system, which
pretends to solve the question of Italian independence, is
absurd. The Pope, whose States are the most miserable
and the worst governed in the Peninsula, put at the head of

the Confederation ! . . . And five thousand lives have been sacrificed for this bad joke ! "

Still another problem, and a much graver in that it required an immediate solution, tormented Napoleon III : the restitution of the Romagnas, of Tuscany, and of the Duchies to their former rulers. Was it possible to credit that these peoples, actually liberated since the war, and whose troops, police, administration, finance, all whose public services, had already been restored to Piedmont, was it possible to credit that they would again accept their detested overseers ? Yet Austria and the Holy See had the right to demand that they should : France had solemnly subscribed to it. More than that, the Treaty of Zurich decreed that the " territorial divisions of Italy could be modified only by those Powers in congress that had originally created them." By this juridical maxim, a curious maxim attributing a kind of collective suzerainty to all the great potentates of Europe, Napoleon III formally renounced the principle of nationality, the primary right of peoples to dispose of themselves. Then what ? . . . Ought he to send a French army to replace Tuscans, the inhabitants of the Romagna, Parma and Modena, in durance vile ? Was France, after having fought for Italy's independence, now to league herself with Austria against Italy ?

Napoleon, as was his custom in difficult situations, tried to extricate himself by sly and confused chicanery. Perhaps in this respect, this was the meanest period of his reign. It is not possible to follow him through the elaboration of intrigue, subterfuge, evasion, counter-march, pretence, connivance, renouncement. Side by side with his official policy, of which Walewski was the harsh interpreter, he pursued several private policies with a swarm of Italian emissaries. Decisions he made in the morning, he reversed in the evening; that which he affirmed to one, he denied to another. Walewski's position in this cacophony soon became untenable. At the end of his patience he wrote to the Emperor: " A sovereign cannot dispense with his ministers. In treating directly either with members of the Diplomatic Corps, or with official and unofficial agents, or with journalists and others, he weakens his prestige; he places the stamp of impotence upon his government's actions; he paralyses the efforts of his own policy. People are seeking to make me pass for a man without character; the Prince Napoleon repeats *ad nauseam* that I altogether ignore what you think and what you do. *The Times* again said, last week, that the commissionaire at the Ministry knows more than I of Your Majesty's policy. The ambassadors, finding the side-door open, pass me by, and in delicate affairs address themselves directly to the Emperor; even our diplomatic agents themselves hesitate; they are not sure if they do right in following my instructions. Do not accuse me of touchiness. I would recall to your mind Plombières, Biarritz; the negotiations with Prussia and Piedmont, all unknown to me; the correspondence in cipher exchanged under my very nose between Prince Napoleon and Turin; the pamphlets and newspaper articles involving your policy worded and drafted without my knowledge; the armistice and the Treaty of Villafranca concluded without even telegraphing to me for form's sake; your correspondence direct with the Pope; your orders to the Duc de Gramont above my head. I say this without rancour : this is treating me neither as a minister nor as a friend ; it is treating me as an inferior."

Not knowing how to extricate himself from this tangle, Napoleon III had recourse to his usual idea—a congress. He invited all the Great Powers shortly to meet in Paris " to come to an arrangement over the means of giving stability and peace to Italy." Hardly had the invitation been issued when he realised that all Europe would be against him and that he was exposing himself to diplomatic catastrophe. So he turned to his old trick : the anonymous pamphlet.

On 22 December a small thinly bound book, just published, appeared in the windows of all booksellers. Its title was *The Pope and the Congress*. A rumour emanating from the Tuileries soon caused the book to be unanimously fathered on Vicomte de la Guéronnière, the habitual mouthpiece of the Imperial revelations. It was a daring composition, and menacing to the Pope. Insinuating, devout, and controlled, the author developed this aphorism : " The Temporal Power is legitimate and necessary ; but it may be limited without the spiritual authority of the Supreme Pontiff being thereby diminished. On the contrary : *the less the territory of the Papal States, the greater their ruler*. Thus Pius IX would be truly inspired were he of his own free will to cut away his rebellious provinces and henceforth confine himself to the city of the Holy Apostles." Molière's physician reasoned thus : " Were I you, Sir, I should cut off my right arm ; the left could be made only stronger if you did so."

This unexpected manifesto, apparently ringing the knell of the Temporal Power, excited lively indignation in all

Catholic countries. Pius IX made a public protest. On
1 January 1860, when receiving the homage and the vows of
Général de Goyon, Officer Commanding the French garrison,
the Pope first called down the blessing of Heaven upon France,
and then, in a ringing and haughty voice already vibrating
with the anger of future denunciation, he added: " We
also pray the Most High that He shed His light upon the
head of this nation so that he may recognise the falsity of
certain principles formulated at this time in a pamphlet that
must be denounced as *a conspicuous monument of hypocrisy and
an infamous fabric of absurdities.*" The Pope soon went even
further; he did not hesitate to say before a large audience:
" The Emperor Napoleon is nothing but a liar and a knave.
I no longer believe his word. Let him leave me alone with
all his hypocritical designs! What power has he over the
Pope? None. Over Mastaï, great. Well, I will take refuge at
the tomb of the Apostle; let him seize me there in my pontifical
robes; but he knows what it means to lay hand on these robes.
For him the hour of justice has struck; the sword of
God in the hands of men is ready to strike him down!"

In Napoleon's crooked mind the publication of the
pamphlet had no other aim than to prevent the assembling
of the Congress; for it was evidently not the time for media-
tory deliberations when controversies were so vehement
on all sides. So that there should be no misunderstanding,
however, the Emperor notified all the Chancelleries of
Europe on 28 December that the Congress was adjourned
sine die. He accepted at the same time Walewski's resignation and replaced him at the Quai d'Orsay by Thouvenel,
his ambassador at Constantinople, a diplomatist no less wise,

but more tractable, more accommodating, and, above all, less nervous.

II

It was at this juncture—20 January—that Cavour was recalled to power.

What would he do? The programme he had sketched out during his lonely cogitations at Léri, and that he of course intended to adapt to circumstances, was one of the prettiest that any statesman had ever conceived. It came under two heads : to rally round the House of Savoy the scattered elements of the Italian nation ; to create thereafter out of this large new group an organic and moral unity by means of the invigorating impulses of free institutions.

For so vast, so long, and therefore so hazardous a task the Piedmontese monarchy had need of foreign support. Here Cavour proved his wisdom. He had not been dazzled by the victories of Magenta and Solferino ; he always saw Austria wedged in south of the Alps, formidably fortified in Verona, Peschiera, Mantua, and Legnago, mistress of the Adriatic through Venice, Trieste, and Pola. Who could tell that she was not secretly meditating revenge ? . . . Six years later Custozza and Lissa justified his strong dread of Austria.

Which should he choose to be his ally: England or France? Since Villafranca the British Government and Press, British opinion, had certainly not grudged their favours to the Italian people. But Cavour knew the traditions of British policy too well to imagine that Britain would risk a vessel or a soldier in the service of a foreign cause outside her vital interests. He would ask only that she give him, and, moreover, give him voluntarily, diplomatic co-operation.

There remained the French alliance. Here again Cavour's vision was very clear. Confused and contradictory as the policy of the Tuileries might be, two facts yet emerged: first, that the Emperor could not again call in question the results of 1859; second, that he who owed his position to the suffrages of the French people could not oppose arms to the effecting of Italian unity. Were not these two facts sufficient for a complete and spacious statecraft to be founded upon the aid, more or less obvious, more or less submissive, of the Imperial Government? Cavour knew Napoleon III well; he knew how to manage him. He set about renewing the French alliance with all possible speed. Hence the hymn to Prince Napoleon: " Blessèd be the peace of Villa-franca ! "

The better to carry out this policy, Cavour appointed his clever secretary Nigra to the Piedmontese Legation in Paris, transferring Villamarina, whom Nigra superseded, to Naples. During his brief missions of 1858 the young diplomat had gained special favour at the Tuileries and in Paris society, and he now proceeded to enhance it. He was soon one of the most marked and most congenial figures at the Imperial Court. Frequenter of drawing-rooms, of *cercles*, and of boudoirs, a brilliant talker, well-mannered, graceful, and even—as Saint-Simon said of the Abbé de Polignac— " of an ingratiating and vigorous eloquence of right words and charming manners, of a fragrant, fine, and pleasing address," he was also skilled in the practice of diplomacy, discerning, compliant, adroit, an adept at surmounting obstacles, at opening doors, at finding expedients, at suggest-ing accommodating formulas, at reconciling principles and necessities : he was well equipped for the delicate part his chief had cast for him.

Hardly were the reins of government again in Cavour's hands when he began to instil a feverish activity into the annexationist manœuvres of Central Italy ; he urged on all his agents at Parma and Modena, at Bologna and Ferrara, at Florence and Leghorn : " Precipitate your disclosures ; redouble your daring ; adopt a menacing tone ! To a few I must be made to look overwhelming."

Protestations soon poured in from Paris. Thouvenel's remonstrances, if less acrimonious than those of Walewski, were not less importunate. But Cavour held in reserve an irresistible argument, a trump card that could not fail to secure France's assent to the territorial aggrandisement on which he was bent. This was the complementary extension of the frontiers of France to the ridge of the Alps, the bringing of Savoy and Nice into the French Empire.

How ʼdid this problem, abandoned since Villafranca, come to be posed anew between the Cabinets of Paris and Turin ? Did Napoleon III renew it ? Was it not rather Cavour who had subtly taken it up again through Nigra or Count Arese during one of their innumerable cabals with the Emperor ? No one knows ; for it is evident that the negotiations were carried on outside official diplomacy. It does not matter. What is beyond doubt, and is sufficient for this purpose to recognise, is Cavour's mental attitude towards the episode. His eagle eye, sweeping the horizon from on high, showed him the whole future of his country at a glance. Rising above actual and transitory contingencies, he realised that the annexation of Central Italy, the first step on the road to Italian unity, was worth much sacrifice ; that the loss of several Transalpine territories would affect neither the security, the wealth, the power, nor the glory of the future Italy. Undaunted, he took the responsibility, as always when momentous action seemed necessary to him.

On 22 March, the settlement being thereafter concluded between Paris and Turin, Victor Emmanuel proclaimed the incorporation of Emilia and Tuscany within the Piedmontese monarchy. Two days later Cavour signed the treaty uniting the province of Savoy and the district of Nice to the French Empire. The annexation would not be definitive until ratified by a plebiscite.

Legal sanction was necessary thus to give up national territory. On 26 May in the Piedmontese Chamber, where for the first time sat representatives of Central Italy, the debate was opened. It was a stormy, a dramatic sitting. All Cavour's enemies, Mazzinians and Clericals, attacked him with extreme violence, reproaching him with having humiliated, having sold, his fatherland. The furious campaign led by Garibaldi against the treaty of cession greatly envenomed the discussion. A native of Nice, he denounced as sacrilege *la vendita vergognosa di Nizza a Napoleone* ; he anathematised the base broker who had traded away his native city. And, since he was not near Cavour, he transfixed him with furious stares " such as one would give a man who had carried off one's mother and sold her in the market-place." The Minister-President addressed the House with dignity and calmness. " This treaty is an integral part of our policy, a logical and inevitable consequence of that policy that guided us formerly at Milan, Bologna

Florence—an absolute necessity for the continuation of this policy in the future." Then in a heated voice he touched on the delicate point: "I say with profound conviction, the cession of Savoy and Nice was indispensable to preserve the amicable sentiments of the French people towards Italy; for, rightly or wrongly, they believe that these provinces belong geographically to France. It was necessary to preserve the French alliance, with which we could not dispense. Do not forget that Italy carries again in her bosom deep wounds. Turn your eyes to Verona and to the Mincio; look at the south of Tuscany, and tell me if Italy has nothing more to fear!" By this frank and vigorous language, this lucid, precise, sound, substantial, free, and conclusive eloquence, the eloquence that Macaulay so much admired in a Burke or a William Pitt, Cavour won over the Assembly; the treaty was ratified on 24 March by an enormous majority.

III

While this grave debate was taking place in Carignan Palace, astounding news had been circulated in Turin and had immediately spread therefrom across a scandalised Europe. On the evening of 5 May, Garibaldi, accompanied by "the Thousand," his most trusted comrades, who had secretly gathered in a suburb of Genoa, seized two vessels, the *Piedmont* and the *Lombardy*, and set out to conquer Sicily. And the Genoese authorities, who saw the whole thing, let them go! Evading the Neapolitan cruisers, the Man in the Red Shirt landed in Marsala on 11 May, and set out on a rapid, breathless, and victorious march to the north of the

17

island. The Bourbon army everywhere fled before him. Several days later, despite ramparts, guns, and 20,000 defenders, the great and flourishing mercantile city of Palermo opened its gates to the *condottiere*. Astonishing prowess, recalling the fine exploits of Norman warrior, Saracen pirate, Scandinavian Viking, carrying the imagination back to legendary times, to the fabulous conquests of the Argonauts ! But in this strange caprice, so vastly exciting to the Italians, so bewildering to the Chancelleries of Europe, the conquering hero but proclaimed intention before all the world : that Palermo marked only a stage, the first stage on that road of glory that after the delivery of Naples, Rome, and Venice, after the setting free of the whole Peninsula, should run from the Adriatic Sea to the Tyrrhenian Sea, from the Gulf of Taranto to the Gulf of Trieste.

The expedition of the Thousand was altogether unexpected by the Italians and by Europe ; it was not by Cavour, who had known of all the preparations. If he had tolerated them, he had at least not furthered them, for he disapproved of the enterprise, deeming it rash, and anticipating that it would call down a storm of diplomatic protest upon the Turin Cabinet, would perhaps offer Napoleon III the opportunity of severing the Piedmontese alliance, and in any case would certainly keep the French in Rome, the very place from which they had shown themselves inclined to withdraw. On the other hand, always careful to balance risks with chances of success and to play all the trumps possible, he would have wished to consolidate the unification of Northern Italy before opening the Neapolitan question on a large scale ; he remembered that " the present position would last several years yet." In order to draw the kingdom of the Two Sicilies into Piedmont's orbit, he sought to form a federative bond, a kind of league, between the Northern and Southern States, a league from which his ready cunning foresaw all kinds of advantages. Garibaldi's action, too, would materially affect the moral character of the *Risorgimento*. Up till now, indeed, the Italian drama had developed in the at least apparent observance of international law. Perfidious and fraudulent as some stealthy acts had been, the official rules of the political game had never once been flagrantly broken. The war of 1859 had been irreproachable from the point of view of juridical correctness. As for the annexations that had followed, they had been carried out without violence : Tuscans, Modenese, Parmesans, Romagnese, had been openly brought under Victor Emmanuel's rule. The attack on Sicily, on the other hand, was indefensible from the point of view of the law of nations, which could regard it only as a signal crime, a monstrous act of brigandage and of piracy. Cavour, then, was energetically opposed to this mad adventure, declaring that if necessity arose he would prevent the departure of the filibusters *manu militari* ; he even meditated Garibaldi's arrest. But Garibaldi had gained for his cause an ally as powerful as unexpected— the King.

Victor Emmanuel's feeling for Garibaldi presents a curious psychological problem. Head of the illustrious House of Savoy, son of the pious Charles Albert, connected through his mother and wife with the Habsburgs, educated in the creed of monarchical principles and traditions, inflexible in questions affecting his prerogatives and his crown, excessively proud of his descent and his coat-of-arms, zealous Christian, scrupulous bigot, he had yet taken a lively fancy to, and conceived a manly affection for, the demagogue of Nice, a poor man's son, a seaman by trade, a captain-adventurer, hostile to all social hierarchies, suspicious of epaulettes, personal enemy of all tyrants, of all police, of all myrmidons, of all custom-house officers; a man more extolled for his " priestophobia " than for his republicanism, who cursed the Pope, calling him " the great impostor, the great Thaumaturgus "; abhorring the Papal Court, which he denounced publicly as " pestilential filth, a cesspool of vileness, a den of hypocrites and charlatans, a cave of foxes and of crocodiles."

Victor Emmanuel's liking for such a man would be inexplicable were it not that a number of indications show that he had a " common " side. Despite his pride of race, he disliked his rôle of monarch except in so far as it had to do with the army. He was interested neither in politics, diplomacy, finance, nor administration. " You don't know," he said once to one of his friends, " you don't know how burdensome my royal livery is ! " So he rebelled against all the restraints of ceremonial, against all the observances of decorous society, and felt himself at ease only when he was with simple peasants and soldiers. This inward propensity seems to lend credence to a legend that was much believed during his infancy : that the real son of Charles Albert had been suffocated in his cradle and had been secretly replaced by a peasant's child. Be that as it may, the fiery roughness of the popular knight-errant appealed to him. What pleased him most of all in the *condottiere* was his patriotism, his

GARIBALDI.

courage, his audacity, his loyalty, his chivalrous spirit, his love of the people, his passion for dangerous, daring, and disinterested adventure. Victor Emmanuel's imagination had taken fire at the idea of the Sicilian expedition, and while the plans were maturing in secret, he had kept in close touch with Garibaldi, unknown to all his ministers, by means of his aides-de-camp; had even written in his own hand to him: " Trust me, and me alone ! "

So Cavour had to let the Argonauts go. And he had quickly perceived how to turn the situation to account. Ostensibly he disowned the adventure of the Thousand, but only so that Piedmont should not lose face in Europe. If the expedition miscarried, so much the worse for the organiser; he would be thrown overboard or shot, as Murat had been in Calabria, and the *Risorgimento* would be eased of this embarrassing Don Quixote, of this " bull in a china-shop " who would not listen to reason. If the expedition succeeded, the Piedmontese Government would change its tactics. Left to themselves, the aggressors would not be able to go very far; they would soon need reinforcements, arms, ammunition, supplies. Then, under pretext of assisting them, Cavour would secretly impose his will on them; he would assign them a programme, place them under orders; he would keep them, willy-nilly, within the limits of official policy.

The surrender of Palermo obliged Cavour to take the affair in hand as early as 6 June. Fortune smiled on Garibaldi, and his prestige was becoming overwhelming throughout the Peninsula; he now was the real leader of the national movement. Italian unity must be brought

about, at any cost, by the people and by revolution only.
Through Piedmont alone must Victor Emmanuel receive
the crown of Italy. The matter was all the more urgent
in that the *condottiere*, who had proclaimed himself dictator
of Sicily, was now using the most intolerable wiles.

Garibaldi's extraordinary victories had developed to the
highest degree his power over the people. He had always
had the gift of moving them, of astounding and fascinating
them. In him the hero and the actor were combined. His
mental powers were slight, but he was crafty; his imagination was scanty, but vivid and picturesque; he possessed in
the highest degree a sense of the dramatic; he knew, none
better, the value of decorativeness and of uniform; he knew
the secret of the striking attitude, the eloquent gesture, the
magnetic gaze; the secret of all the trivial and ordinary
acts that win over and dominate the crowd. In the eyes of
the Sicilians he had become a kind of Messiah since his landing
at Marsala. His calmness in the thick of the fight, his cheer-
fulness in extreme danger, made him appear invulnerable,
and it was said that he had many a time been seen carelessly
shaking from the folds of his great cloak the bullets about
to riddle it. Lord of a worshipping Palermo, he had at
once stripped himself of his ferocious anti-clericalism to be
present at a pontifical Mass in the old cathedral of solemn
memories. There, in his red shirt, exalted on a throne,
awarded the honours of an apostolic legate, sitting as stiff
as a poker, eyes flashing in an inspired face, he had unsheathed
his sword during the reading of the Gospel as the Norman
Kings, appointed champions of Holy Church, had been
used to do.

Cavour therefore had no time to lose if he would remain the guiding principle in the national movement. And then it was necessary for him to send immediately, with the at least feigned co-operation of the Piedmontese squadron, the reinforcements that the dictator was so vigorously demanding; for a Neapolitan army, thirty thousand strong, was about to cross the Straits of Messina in an effort to recapture Palermo. Meanwhile an avalanche of diplomatic protestations had descended upon the Royal Government at Turin, who were no longer able to deny complicity in the Sicilian adventure. Austria, Russia, and Prussia accused Piedmont of being the hardened disturber of the European order and talked of nothing less than of teaching her by force of arms the respect due her international obligations. France too protested. Even England began to dread the consequences of the Garibaldian raid that she had found pleasing enough at first; she charged her minister, Sir James Hudson, to confide her uneasiness to Cavour. " Well, what can we do? " asked Cavour. " Do you not see that the flower of Italian youth all over the country are flocking to Garibaldi's standard? If the King's Government tried to crush this national transport, it would crush itself, and that would mean the triumph, throughout the length and breadth of the Peninsula, of Mazzinians, republicans, anarchists—of the mob. Does Europe want that? . . . Believe me, if the torrent of revolutionary ideas is to be checked and guided, the House of Savoy must continue to hold that moral authority it acquired when it placed itself at the head of the *Risorgimento*. We deplore Garibaldi's adventure; we are not aiding in it; do not ask us to combat it."

While the Piedmontese minister thus played his hand as prudently as possible, and strove to show spirit in the face of the censures and menaces of European diplomacy, the Southern Italian drama suddenly took a grave turn. The royalist army that was to have conquered Sicily was ignominiously beaten at Milazzo. Garibaldi prepared to pass into Calabria and to march on Naples.

This was perhaps the period in Cavour's alternating fortunes when his political genius showed itself most acute, most supple, and most daring.

The victory of Milazzo was so signal that the victor had to be congratulated; but, " God willing, Garibaldi won't get ahead of us at Naples," was a cry from Cavour's inmost heart. He telegraphed to Admiral Persano, commanding the Piedmontese squadron : " Use your utmost skill to hold back, on any pretext whatsoever, the passage of the Garibaldians into Calabria. Do your best for the great aim we have before us : *to organise Italy without allowing ourselves to be dominated by revolution.*" To outstrip revolution, he borrowed revolution's own methods—violence, deceit, charlatanism, bribery, imposture ; he did away with scruple and decency ; for he would try for nothing less than the overthrow of the throne of Naples, so that Garibaldi, when he arrived, should find the royal House of Savoy already installed at the foot of Vesuvius. On 30 July Cavour ordered Admiral Persano to proceed to Naples and to confer immediately with Villamarina, formerly Victor Emmanuel's minister at Paris and now accredited to Francis II : these were the direct mediums, the principal organs, of the vast conspiracy he had just conceived ; to them he added several intrepid emissaries whom he had supplied with much hard cash. One of these was the young Marquis Visconti-Venosta.

Disaster came swift and sudden. There were violent demonstrations before the *Palazzo Reale*, processions in thronged streets, inflammatory speeches, provocative placards, mutinies in barracks, intrigues and conspiracies even in the royal family. It was well-nigh incredible that all these had been planned, controlled, furthered, by an ardent loyalist, by the First Minister of one of the oldest monarchies in Europe. Yet, Cavour could have said, had the great players of the game of politics, Richelieu, Mazarin, Cromwell, William of Orange, Frederick II, Napoleon I, Metternich, had they been checked by a moral law? Once for all Machiavelli had laid down the rule of the game of founding and saving empires when, as a penetrating observer and strict logician, he had declared with imperturbable coolness that honour, justice, and virtue have nothing to do with affairs of State; that success justifies all means; that fraud and villainy are some-times necessary to the welfare and prosperity of peoples; in short, when he wrote: " A wise mind never condemns a man who in the loftier interests of his fatherland has had to have recourse to singular acts."

Yet, whatever the zeal of Persano, Villamarina, and their acolytes might have been, the Neapolitan populace reacted but nervelessly. It gesticulated, it speechified, it bawled itself hoarse—but it did not revolt. Energetically worked from below by Mazzinian agents, it awaited " the Red Man," it demanded Garibaldi. Cavour's propaganda was most efficacious in the family and household of the King. Soon the unfortunate Francis II was surrounded by traitors : his very uncles, the Counts of Syracuse, Trapani, and d'Aquila, went over to the enemy. On 5 September he learned that the Garibaldians, passing from victory to victory, were already nearing Salerno. Then, feeling himself indeed lost, he embarked for Gaeta, accompanied by his brave wife, the beautiful, smooth and secret Maria Sophia of Bavaria. In Gaeta he concentrated the few troops remaining faithful to him.

Cavour's conspiracy had miscarried. The Red Man was on the point of entering Naples before the flag bearing the white cross of Savoy had been hoisted on the castle of St. Elmo. Garibaldi entered Naples on 7 September in the midst of hysterical acclamations. An immense crowd of all classes and opinions, Mazzinians and Camorrists, artisans and bourgeoisie, patriots and clericals, priests and Capuchins, ruffians and lazerones, escaped convicts, women of fashion in flowered corsages, women of the people with mops of frizzled hair, even the fair and venomous pretty ladies of the *Porta Capuana*—a whole population, excited, vociferous, convulsed, thronged disorderly about their hero, whose first act was to repair to the cathedral, where—a miracle !—the blood of St. Januarius instantly, inevitably, liquefied in the sacred vial.

On the morrow, still intoxicated with his triumph, Garibaldi solemnly announced that he would march on Rome without delay. He did not hesitate to inform the English minister, Sir Henry Elliot, who immediately objected : " March on Rome ! . . . Do you think of doing that ? . . . And the French garrison ? " " Well, what about it ? "

replied the dictator, ablaze. " Rome is an Italian town, and neither the Emperor Napoleon himself nor anyone else in the world has the right to refuse me entry. If the French resist me, I shall chase them out. . . . In any case, I shall not delay in Rome. When I have proclaimed Victor Emmanuel King of Italy, I shall go back to the north, attack the Austrians, deliver Venice, and not stop until I have freed the whole Peninsula ! "

It was a critical moment for Cavour. What could he do ? After all that he had dared, what more could he dare ? Yet he did not hesitate an instant. He had foreseen the crisis that had developed ; he had at least considered its development possible. Since 1 August, when the victory of Milazzo had enabled the Garibaldians to penetrate into Calabria, he had evolved a new plan to meet the case if they reached Naples before the Piedmontese monarchy had taken possession of it.

This plan, deeply meditated in secret, established with minute exactitude, much surpassed in daring Garibaldi's landing at Marsala. The *condottiere*, if he had failed, had merely risked being shot. But the head of the Piedmontese Government, by playing this hand, would stake not only his personal reputation but also the honour and the fate of his country on its success. The greatness of the interests at stake, the imminence of the danger, the national necessity, nevertheless justified his boldness. His acute mind perceived that the prodigious successes of the Red Man would make for the promotion of Piedmontese hegemony in the Peninsula, and he exclaimed to his friends : " The Savoyard dynasty cannot tolerate that the *Risorgimento* be consummated by a mere *condottiere*. It must itself gain all that remains to be gained. To establish its prestige in Southern Italy, to connect the South with the North, it must open up a road across the Papal States, invade the Marches and Umbria, push on to Naples, attack the Bourbon troops in their stronghold at Gaeta, if they are still capable of fighting, and thus reduce Garibaldi to the only position to which he has the right to pretend—that of the daring adventurer." But to invade without the least provocation, and in piping times of peace, a territory sacred in the eyes of all the Catholic world, a territory safeguarded by the French flag, the Papal territory, was an act so heinous, so charged with gravity politically and morally, that before actually determining upon it, Cavour at least wished to secure himself with France. In reality, he had an eye on Vienna. Would not this dangerous adventure that he was about to undertake, and all the complications necessarily arising therefrom—would not they offer Austria a plausible pretext for revenging herself for Solferino and reconquering Lombardy? He could do nothing without the at least tacit consent of France. "We cannot dispense with France," he said, "for without her we should be at the mercy of Austria."

At that instant Napoleon III visited his new provinces. On 28 August he was at Chambéry, where Victor Emmanuel sent Farini, Minister of the Interior, and General Cialdini, to wait upon him. Before they left, Cavour made known his plan to the two envoys, charging them to disclose it to the Emperor.

IV

The unhappy Napoleon III had had very little pleasure during the last few months out of his omnipotence. Not a single satisfaction and many a gloomy thought—capricious Fortune had not once smiled on him. In the first place, the innumerable worries caused him by the annexations in Central Italy had completely dispelled his Italian illusions. At times, as Prince Albert wrote, " he would have liked to see the Peninsula at the bottom of the Mediterranean." He thought of nothing but of withdrawing his troops from Rome, of settling the obnoxious Roman Question as well as he could.

On the other hand, there weighed on him the feeling that every European Court was suspicious of him. No one believed his word any longer; everyone was asking himself what Napoleon III was hatching now, what new move was to be expected from him. This universal suspicion troubled him even more than it offended him, for the shadow of his charitable mysticism, the perpetual irresolution of his spirit, the contradictory play of his intrigues and his pledges, prevented his seeing that he deceived everyone. He even sincerely believed himself loyal.

A curious witness to the state of his mind at this period is a letter he sent on 25 July to Persigny, his ambassador at London, and that he inserted shortly after in the papers as a kind of open confession. It runs : " Thanks to the mistrust everywhere excited since the Italian war, matters seem to me to be so complicated that I am writing to you in the hope

that a perfectly frank conversation with Lord Palmerston
will serve to remedy this evil.   Lord Palmerston knows me,
and believes a thing when I tell it him.   Well, you can tell
him from me that, since the Peace of Villafranca, I have had
but one aim : to live on the best possible terms with all my
neighbours and especially with England.   But, in Heaven's
name, do secure that the eminent men who are at the head
of his Government, put this unjust suspicion aside !   Let us
work frankly, loyally, one with another like the honest
people that we are, and not like scamps who try to deceive
each other."   Several days later Napoleon took up the
matter with Lord Clarendon, who was passing through Paris.
" Why," he asked Lord Clarendon, " why has England no
longer confidence in me ? "   The old lord replied plainly :
" Because all the declarations Your Majesty has made to us
have been repudiated the next day ; because your policy of
brusque right-about-face creates universal uneasiness ; because
everyone every morning asks himself what new surprise you
have prepared for the world overnight."   " Well, what
then ? . . .   There is nothing for me to do but to retire
into my shell and compensate myself for everything ! "
" Nothing would be wiser, and if only Your Majesty would
persevere in this resolution, confidence in Your Majesty
would quickly return."

Napoleon III had had an even graver cause for uneasiness
and gloom ever since the amazing vagaries of the Garibaldians in Sicily.   He easily resigned himself to the annexations
in Central Italy, since France profited by them to the extent
of Nice and Savoy.   Could he accept the annexation of the
Kingdom of Naples by Piedmont, seeing that no counterpart

had been bargained for in this hypothesis? As at Plombières, he dreamed always of an Italy divided into three parts, " a kingdom of the north, a kingdom of the south, with the pontifical sovereignty between the two." But here all of a sudden was an adventurer foolishly attempting to effect Italian unity. What degradation for the power of France! . . . Prince Napoleon himself was dismayed. " Are we," he said, " going to allow a great nation to be set up at our very door, a great nation of twenty-five million people, grouped about a secular dynasty? Are we going thus to sacrifice the ancient influence that France has exerted over the Latin races? "

Certainly Napoleon III could easily rescue the kingdom of Naples: it would suffice to send a peremptory *veto* to Turin, emphasised by the dispatch of a squadron to the Straits of Messina. But when Francis II had implored his help, he had replied to the Neapolitan ambassador: " My position is exceedingly difficult. One cannot check a revolution with words. The Italians are wary: they would never believe that, after having spilled the blood of my soldiers for Italian independence, I would train my guns upon it." Since then, following his natural inclinations, he had, instead of acting, sunk himself in the silence of his nebulous and fatalistic reflections. He was thus in a state of considerable depression when on 28 August Victor Emmanuel's envoys came to greet him at Chambéry.

Duly trained by Cavour, and after a long interview with Dr. Conneau (who was thus able to warn his master), Farini and General Cialdini expounded to the Emperor the pressing reasons that obliged the Piedmontese Government to invade the Papal territory. "We cannot allow revolution to triumph at Naples. To re-establish order we must occupy the Marches and Umbria; but we shall not meddle with the province of Rome. Our military dispositions are already taken: the movement will be accomplished in several days." Napoleon III listened without interrupting. Then he said in his slow way: "My position will not be very agreeable. . . . Diplomacy will raise an uproar. . . . I must propose another congress." Not a word in protest against the morality of the enterprise proposed to him, against the enormity of this crime against common right. The Emperor expressed curiosity only concerning the programme of the strategic operations, and when he was informed of it, he smiled at the idea of the Papal soldiery being obliged to fight. The audience was short. When Victor Emmanuel's envoys rose to take their leave, the Emperor, affable and courteous as ever, said in shaking hands, "Good luck; but be quick about it!"

Not a single original French document exists concerning this famous interview at Chambéry—an interview too similar to that at Plombières. Recourse must be had to the testimony of the Piedmontese envoys, who have, however, not varied in their accounts of it. Yet several historians have refused to believe that the Emperor subscribed thus easily to the spoliation of the Pope; above all that he gave utterance to the final phrase: "Good luck; but be quick about it!" Their opinion has against it at least the whole succession of events. It is noteworthy, besides, that as early as 4 September —seven days before the invasion of the Papal States—the Duc de Gramont, ambassador at Rome, had telegraphed to

Paris : " Following a correspondence with Berlin, the Emperor, when receiving at Chambéry the envoys of King Victor Emmanuel, willingly consented to Piedmont's annexing the territory of the Church, provided the Pope would be maintained in the Eternal City." But Napoleon III sent no contradiction to Rome, and demanded no explanation from Turin. It was only on 23 September, when the " crime of Chambéry " had been effected and the Piedmontese outrage had roused the choler of all Europe, that Thouvenal telegraphed to Gramont : " The Emperor denounces Piedmont's policy as vehemently as we do. He is shocked at the means employed to suggest that he had said a word that could lead M. de Cavour to believe himself encouraged or countenanced in his vile adventure." There is another argument still more decisive. If Napoleon III had not consented to the invasion of the Papal States, the most elementary prudence would have caused him to occupy Ancona and Perugia with the French division garrisoned in Rome ; this move, a simple measure of internal order, would have safeguarded the domain of the Church. But he had carefully retained his troops on the banks of the Tiber while the little Papal army, this caricature of an army at which he had smiled at Chambéry, had been alone at grips with the aggressors. Finally, in an excess of caution and to make certain of Napoleon's acquiescence, Cavour had on 31 August dispatched to the Emperor at Thonon Count Arese, the great friend of Cavour's revolutionary youth, the friend with whom he had then waged war in this Romagna in which " the vile adventure " was about to be engaged. This time again the Emperor had been " perfect." He had even, in order to

18

avoid importunate argument with his ministers, left immediately for Algeria.

On 11 September, on the vague pretext of re-establishing order in the Apennine district, fifteen Piedmontese divisions, 45,000 men, invaded the Marches and Umbria. The Papal army of 20,000 men, badly organised and as badly led, broke up and disappeared as it were of itself before this invasion, at Perugia, Orvieto, Foligno, Spoleto. On 18 September it broke up finally at Castelfidardo. Several days later its brave leader, La Moricière, hero of Constantine and of Mouzaïa, who had come " to flourish the sacred banner of Lepanto against the savages of the nineteenth century," was compelled to capitulate at Ancona. Thereafter the road to Naples lay open.

Now comes the epilogue to the drama, in which Cavour displayed neither less agility nor less skill. A double task, of extreme urgency, confronted him. It was necessary that the House of Savoy should, in the person of its head, take immediate possession of Southern Italy, and at the same time it was necessary to deal with Garibaldi.

On 3 October Victor Emmanuel arrived at Ancona to assume the command of his army. He was happy to be again in the midst of his soldiers, to waken at dawn to the sounding of the réveillé, to have incessantly in his ears the sound of trumpet and drum, not to have a single stupid paper to read, and to be in the saddle from morning to night. So that nothing should spoil his pleasure he took with him the fair Rosine, who, anxious to cut a fine figure on this warlike expedition, adorned herself with her most brilliant jewels and most startling frocks. Yet he was melancholy too, for he was a good Catholic, and the Pope was excommunicating him as a despoiler of the Church, " adjuring princes and peoples to pray that assistance might be given the Vicar of Christ against the murderous armies of a degenerate son." Somewhat to mitigate his remorse, Victor Emmanuel told himself that he was but a passive instrument in the hand of God, that this sort of thing would not happen without Heaven being accessory to it. " How," said he to his intimates, " how can we believe that all this is not part of God's design, since, in spite of so many errors and so many faults, we have had nothing but success ? " A favourite formula of consolation and resignation with the pious Louis XI was : " After all, it was the will of Providence ! "

Matters soon settled themselves. On 7 October the army was set in motion. The King made a short halt at Loretto, where he did not fail to go to pray before the *Santissima Casa* of the Virgin. As he left the wonderful church, his emotions deeply touched, his eyes still dazzled by the radiance of the shrines and tabernacles, he was seized by a desire to offer 50,000 francs to the Bishop. " Beware, Sire," insinuated his aide-de-camp ; " he will not accept it." The gift was accepted with joy, and a few moments later the Bishop was breakfasting with the King.

On 26 October Victor Emmanuel encountered Garibaldi near Capua on the Volturno, where his heroic troops were about to engage and to repulse towards Gaeta the troops remaining faithful to Francis II. On horseback, in black cap and red shirt, a large silk scarf about his neck, the knight-errant came at the trot towards the King. Then, raising his cap in the air, he cried : " Hail, King of Italy ! " Victor

Emmanuel held out his hand. " Hail, beſt of my friends ! "
They conversed cordially ; they rode side by side. " What
is the ſtate of your troops ? " asked the King. " Very tired,
Sire." " That is not surprising, considering how long they
have fought ! My own troops are quite fresh ; yours can
reſt." Several days later, when the Piedmontese army
occupied Naples, the Red Man was told that his part had
been played, that there was no further need of his services.
Vićtor Emmanuel offered him rewards : the Order of the
Annunciation, a caſtle, an endowment, a ducal title. He
would have none of them. On 9 November he sailed for
his sea-girt crag of Caprera, avoiding all public demonſtration,
with bloodshot and angry eyes, a flame in his breaſt, an evil
and unbridled tongue ; yet great and fine at this moment of
his life, for after six months of uncontrolled dićtatorship he
carried away with him nothing but a sack of flour, a box of
red herring, four crowns, a morsel of cheese, and a small
cruſt of bread.

CHAPTER IX

FROM VICTORY TO DEATH

CHAPTER IX

FROM VICTORY TO DEATH

I

AT the end of the year 1860 Cavour, taking his daily walk under the arcades of the Via del Po, met d'Ideville, Secretary to the French Legation, a man whom he liked. He took his arm and walked him along with him. Cavour questioned d'Ideville closely upon current affairs, examined and sounded him; slipped into unguarded talk of Napoleon III; then, shaking his head in friendly disapproval, said: " Ah! your Emperor will never change! . . . Where he is wrong is in always wishing to plot. But God knows what need he has to plot now! Is he not the supreme master? What has he to fear with a powerful country like yours, a large army, Europe at peace? Why does he always, every minute, mask his thoughts, turn to the right when he wants to turn to the left, and vice versa? . . . What a splendid conspirator he is! " D'Ideville objected timidly: " Are you not a little severe, M. le Comte? Were you yourself not once a valiant conspirator? " " I? Yes, of course I used to plot . . . but because I had to, because we were not then the most powerful. Whereas who is there to-day to prevent your Emperor openly going straight to his mark? . . . Yet no, he prefers to confuse people and to draw red herrings across his trail. . . . He is a born plotter, and will always be one ! "

This language, smacking strongly of the truth, shows clearly that trait in Cavour that distinguished him so sharply from Napoleon III : an instinctive faculty for adapting himself to circumstances, an almost involuntary compliance to the necessities of the case, an ease, an elasticity, a complete flexibility in the exercise of that function in which above all others the statesman is discovered : the manipulation of facts.

Cavour had plotted, in very truth. He had done nothing but plot for two years, and with what daring, what abandon, what contempt for moral laws ! Yet he had plotted then because plotting had been imposed upon him. The situation was different now ; other methods were necessary : he plotted no more. Henceforth his diplomacy would be irreproachable, immaculate, straightforward, academic.

A new era had opened in the history of the *Risorgimento*. Two leading questions, the one as ticklish and involved, as burning and formidable, as the other, confronted the Piedmontese Government : the question of Venice ; the question of Rome. It was impossible to avoid them ; for that imbecile of a Garibaldi, in his glittering perorations at Naples, had declared and declared again that he of his own strength was prepared to solve them both by the irresistible reasoning of his red-shirted volunteers.

The two cases were not entirely similar. Venice was in the hands of Austria, who, in addition to her strong position on the Mincio, had just laid the foundations of a political agreement, perhaps even of a military alliance, with Prussia and Russia, during mysterious cabals at Warsaw. It was easy to believe, then, that if Piedmont were mad enough to invade Venetia, the occurrence would not be passed over as had that of Castelfidardo. With courageous honesty Cavour had refused to allow the Venetian question to be opened. "Lively as is our affection for Venice," he openly declared in Parliament, "for Venice the great martyr, we must realise that war with Austria would be impossible actually, impossible because we lack military resources, impossible because we should have all the Powers against us. . . . Then what can we do ? Resign ourselves to applying to the public opinions of France, England, Germany, to enlightening, to converting them. And when the truth is known to them, the pitiable fate of Venice will inspire pity of such sort in them that our object will be near to attainment. Will deliverance be achieved by arms or by diplomacy ? I pass that over : it is in the lap of the gods." Behold, then, the question of Venice shelved ; but the principle of a future demand, the irrevocable rights of an *Italia irredenta*, were solemnly proclaimed before Europe.

As far as Rome was concerned, Cavour already foresaw a possible solution, and one that excluded any violent action. For it was evident that the prompt methods that had been applied with so much success in the Romagna, the Marches, and Umbria, could not be applied to the remainder of the Papal States, above all to the Eternal City over which floated the French flag. Cavour's extremely daring plan was no less than personally to negotiate with the Holy See a voluntary renunciation on the part of the Pope of his political and temporal sovereignty. That this plan should have been determined on by the Piedmontese minister is almost beyond belief, for his maladroit anticlericalism of the past, the horror he had inspired in the whole Papal Court, the dreadful thunders of the Church against him as despoiler and sacrilegist, were scarcely a qualification for so delicate a negotiation. But the subject was opened so dexterously; the suggestions that emanated from Turin placed it upon so high a level; indicated so broad a spirit; so profound a respect for religious sentiment; so firm a resolution of guaranteeing the Holy Father the complete independence of his spiritual power with all the rights, honours, and prerogatives, all the grace appertaining to the highest sovereignty, that the negotiations rapidly took on a favourable aspect. Moreover, in the person of the Jesuit Father Passaglia, among other willing agents, Cavour had found a most subtle and sagacious spokesman, one who had lately acquired the affection of Pius IX by his fine doctrinal polemics in favour of the Immaculate Conception. Little is known of the detail of the negotiations. But it is known that several powerful members of the College of Cardinals, including Cardinal Antonelli, principal political adviser to the Pope, had approved the proposed arrangement. Enough progress had been made by 21 February 1861 to enable Cavour to write to Father Passaglia : " I hope that before Easter you will send me an olive branch, symbol of a perpetual peace between Church and State, between the Papacy and the Italian people. If this comes to pass, the joy of the Catholic world will be greater than that which, nearly nineteen hundred years ago, greeted the entrance into Jerusalem of our Saviour." The matter

POPE PIUS IX.

was settled a few weeks later, and specific formulas submitted to the Pope. Suddenly, on 21 March, the whole thing collapsed. The Cardinals, after having warmly supported the negotiations, recanted; Cavour's willing agents, and even Father Passaglia himself, were banished from Rome. What had happened? No one knew. Had there been merely a violent protest on the part of reactionary cardinals, a protest fomented by the truculent Mgr de Mérode, fearless champion of Ultramontane autocracy? Had there not also been one of those sinuous and profitable intrigues by which Cardinal Antonelli allowed himself to be led astray too often for his perfect resemblance to Mazarin? There was nothing to go upon but theories. From that day forth Pius IX stubbornly defended his temporal power. As long as he lived he did not cease to promulgate the absolute incompatibility between Papal independence and Italian unity. " They dispute me this grain of sand under my feet," he exclaimed; " they will not dislodge me from it. This corner of the earth is mine; I received it from Christ; to Him alone will I render it again." His distress was so great that on the morning of 2 April, during his Mass, he was seen suddenly to collapse on his throne; motionless, his face paler than his robes, his eyes dull and holding the shadows of death, he was conspicuous before the world and men—*spectaculum facti sumus mundo et hominibus.*

This abrupt *volte-face* on the part of the Papal Court was a catastrophe for Cavour. Yet he recovered himself almost immediately, resilient as ever. As on the morrow of Villafranca, he told himself: " I followed one course. It was stopped. Well, I will follow another."

He discovered his other course forthwith. He had not been able to make Pius IX of his own free will lay aside his temporal crown. Very well, he would now try to induce Napoleon III to withdraw his troops from Rome. For on that day when the Papacy was no longer protected by French bayonets, the Romans would speedily revolt against the Papal theocracy, and would claim their incorporation into the Italian kindred. He did not doubt that this clever scheme, if clothed in becoming formulas, would appeal to the Tuileries. In point of fact, diplomatic relations between the Imperial Government and the Vatican had been extremely strained since Castelfidardo. The position of the ambassador, Gramont, was hardly tenable any longer. " I am living in an atmosphere of aversion and suspicion," he wrote. Even the Commandant of the French garrison, General de Goyon, a very godly man, received compliments of this kind from Mgr de Mérode : " You are the most tarnished piece of the tinsel with which your master covers his baseness ! " The Emperor would accept with alacrity any expedient that would allow him to adjust with the least prejudice the errors of his Roman policy.

His scheme thoroughly explained to Paris, Cavour resolutely aired the question of the Temporal Power in Parliament. With a freedom and exaltation his speech had never before attained, he proclaimed that Rome must and would be the capital of Italy ; but he added : " We wish to go to Rome without causing mortification to France who is in occupation there, or the Holy See that resides there. Even were France in no position to contest our entry into the Eternal City, we should still not wish to enter it without her consent. Let the maintenance of the integrity of the Papal State cost what it must to the independence of the Sovereign Pontiff, we yet consider it would be not less fatal to Italy than to Catholicism. . . . This is what we shall say to the Pope : ' Holy Father, the Temporal Power is no guarantee of your independence ; renounce it. In exchange we shall give you those spiritual exemptions that the Papacy has vainly claimed for centuries from all the Catholic Powers and of which it has with difficulty obtained a few scraps by means of concordats that but shackle itself. We offer you these exemptions freely, fully, unconditionally ; we proclaim *a free Church in a free State*, and we shall inscribe this principle among the primary decrees of the kingdom.' I am confident that the generous spirit of Pius IX will not cast away the imperishable glory of having reconciled the Italian nation with the Church, Religion with Liberty ! "

At the same time Cavour was negotiating with the Tuileries by means of Prince Napoleon the bases of a convention engaging that France should withdraw her troops from Rome and that Italy should guarantee not to attack the actual domain of the Holy See. The bases were soon agreed upon.

II

These negotiations, serious in that they were a tacit prelude to the destruction of the Papal theocracy, were yet but a detail of the Prime Minister's overwhelming efforts. Besides his diplomatic work, the whole internal organisation of the new Italy rested upon his shoulders—that is to say, the administrative assimilation of the recently acquired provinces ; the fusion of their dissimilar laws and customs ; the co-ordination of their economic, fiscal, financial, custom-house, and other systems. All this quite apart from the tranquillising of the Southern Peninsula where the demagogic ideas of the Red Man had left behind them rebellion, anarchy, brigandage, and ruin. It would still be impossible exactly to estimate the difficulty of Cavour's task, if it were not remembered to what extent, since the most remote times, since the break-up of the Carlovingian Empire, Italy had always been particularist and Ghibelline, unsympathetic to centralisation, impervious to the modern principle of great unified states. The liberal spirit shown by Cavour in this immense work of national construction and social consolidation adds greatly to his lustre. It was suggested to him from several quarters that he should assume the powers of a dictator, but with cheerful dignity he replied : " I have no confidence at all in dictators ; I think that with a parliament one can do many things impossible for an absolute power. A thirteen years' experience has convinced me that a faithful and active minister, who has nothing to fear from parliamentary disclosure and who is not of a disposition to be intimidated by party violence, has all to gain from parliamentary contests. I have never felt myself so powerless as when Parliament was closed. Moreover, I cannot betray my beginnings, or renounce my life-long principles. I am a son of Liberty ; I owe all that I am to her."

Cavour's enemies did not fail to turn his Liberalism to account against him. One fine April morning the Red Man unexpectedly landed at Genoa. The electors of Naples were about to nominate him as deputy. His retreat to Caprera, far from quenching him, had only increased his arrogance, aggravated his malice, inflamed his insatiable appetite for melodramatic adventure. Seething with anger, spouting fire and flame, he demanded resplendent rewards for his companions in glory; he trumpeted that the hour was come for Italy to rise from a low and vulgar state to that of " an armed nation "; finally he denounced as traitors to their country " Cavour and all the false flunkeys who served him in his villainous policy." These ebullitions sent the temperature of the country from Turin to Palermo up to fever-point. It almost seemed that it was on the verge of civil war.

Questions were asked in Parliament on 18 April. But Cavour did not take up the challenge : it was Baron Bettino Ricasoli, the former dictator of Florence, who of all Cavour's compatriots resembled him most in sturdiness of spirit and sense of authority, who began the duel. Patrician of ancient lineage, harsh of eye, thin of lip, bony of chin, rigid in figure, distant in manner, he hid behind this chilling exterior the most generous and passionate of souls. His face had so much the appearance of being embossed, his features were so pronounced and so strongly individual, that it seemed that one had seen them before among representations of Dante or on a medallion by Pisanello. He crushed Garibaldi in a few telling words. " Who then," he cried, " after these times just past, who then dares to arrogate to himself the prerogatives of patriotism and of disinterestedness ? Who claims to be exalted above all others ? One head alone has the right to rule us, that of the King. . . . It is Victor Emmanuel who made our nation; he is our liberator. Let it be enough for us to march behind so noble a leader and to be able to say to ourselves: ' In serving him we serve our country well!'" During this eloquent exhortation that held the whole assembly breathless, Cavour murmured in his neighbour's ear: " Now I know what true eloquence is." Then, always practical, he added: " If I die to-morrow, there stands my successor!"

Compelled to ascend the tribune in his turn, Garibaldi writhed in a tangle of laborious and untaught phrases. To the despair of his supporters, who had invaded the upper galleries, he could neither extricate himself nor be silent. He nevertheless found enough words to cover with insult " the man who had made him a foreigner in Italy, the miserable creature who had sold Nice and Savoy to Napoleon!"

When the storm evoked by these last words had somewhat subsided, the Prime Minister, dreadfully pale under the flood of insult, replied: " I know that a gulf has opened between General Garibaldi and myself. It was a sad duty, the most grievous in my life, to counsel the King to approve the cession of Savoy and of Nice to France. The sadness that filled me then teaches me what General Garibaldi is suffering now, and if he will not forgive me for that necessary act, I shall not reproach him." Then, rising above personal enmities, he sketched in a masterly manner the broad outlines of his policy. A motion inspired by these ideas brought the debate to a conclusion.

III

In the days following Cavour showed extreme languor. His friend, Count de Salmour, was disturbed at his death-like pallor, and on 26 May Cavour said to him : " I am not feeling well. I cannot get over that horrible wrangle with Garibaldi. . . . But never mind—I must get on ; the country needs me." The next day and until 29 May he took part in several very lively debates on internal policy and customs reform. Then he rapidly grew worse, showing all the symptoms of the noxious marsh-fever : ague with great fluctuations of temperature, bilious sickness, deliriums, algidity. He had already had several attacks of this disease, which he had first contracted in the rice-fields at Léri, and his vigorous constitution had always triumphed easily. But now his physical resistance was exhausted by three years of arduous work, of really Herculean labour—from which he had too often sought rest in the arms of Omphale.

On the morning of 5 June his favourite niece, the Marchioness Alfieri, whom he liked to have by his bedside constantly, said to him : " Uncle, Father Giacomo has come to see how you are. Would you like to see him for a moment ? " Cavour stared at her. He understood. " Let him come in," he said. Then he asked to be left alone with the priest.

Father Giacomo, a Franciscan, was the Vicar of St. Mary of Angels, Cavour's parish. His entry into the dying man's presence raised before the priest's conscience a very grave and solemn problem, for not only had Cavour ceased from his youth to practise religion, but on 25 March 1860 he had

19

been included in the Pope's major excommunication of
" all the authors, promoters, advisers, or accomplices of
the crime committed against the Holy See by the usurpation
of the Romagnas." The Franciscan was therefore prepared
for the secret drama that was to be enacted between the
dying man and himself. In 1856 Cavour had made him
promise to support him *in articulo mortis*.

On the day on which this promise had been given,
Cavour's friend, Count de Salmour, visiting his friend, had
found him unusually alert and cheerful. " Camille," he
said, " you are lively enough this morning to have done a
good stroke of business." " I have. The best business
of my life. I have just had my priest's (Father Giacomo)
word that when I summon him to my death-bed he will
come to administer the Sacrament to me without demanding
of me anything I could not honourably consent to." " Is
that all the joke ? But you are sound, hearty, in the prime
of life ; you have plenty of time yet for these religious
precautions." " No, I'm not joking. But I have no
desire to find myself in the position of poor Santa-Rosa,
to whom Christian burial was refused because he would
not sign a retraction of the part he played when the ecclesiastical laws were being voted upon, a retraction he thought
contrary to his sense of honour. I do not want to expose
myself to a like scandal. I am a Catholic, and I want to
die in my religion. And then you must not forget that my
grandmother belonged to the family of St. Francis de Sales.
. . . But now I am happy. My priest is a saint and an honour-
able man : he will keep his promise. And that's why I am
so cheerful this morning ! "

Alone with Cavour, Giacomo confessed him, absolved him, and gave him the Viaticum, without requiring him to disown the sacrileges that brought him excommunication. The Franciscan was soon called to account in Rome for this action. Pius IX, generally so benignly paternal, reproached him harshly for not having imposed an unqualified retraction on his penitent before committing him to Christ. With inflexible determination of character and principle the monk refused to vindicate himself by pleading the sacred secrecy of the confessional. Arraigned the following day before the inquisitors of the Holy Office, he persisted in his courageous attitude ; he steadfastly refused to disclose the private information given him when he forgave the dying man his sins, and pronounced the holy words over his parting soul. The trial did not last long. Forbearingly, and perhaps also *ad evitandum scandalum majus*, Father Giacomo was allowed by his terrible judges to return to Turin, but was declared unworthy for the future of ministering to a parish. As for Cavour—what impulses had he obeyed, what was his secret mood, when he had called the Vicar of St. Mary of Angels to his bedside ?

Without any desire to penetrate the secret that the Franciscan—its sole guardian—had refused to deliver up to the Pope, the historian and the moralist have yet the right to put the question that had already been put concerning the confession *in extremis* of another excommunicated and no less illustrious man : Talleyrand. To-day everything of Talleyrand's confession is known : all the manœuvring by means of delay, finesse, subterfuge, to which the great dissembler had recourse before consenting to sign " the

19*

treaty of peace offered him by the most merciful king in the world." In Cavour there was nothing of this: he was frankness, sincerity, itself. It is noteworthy that he did not wait until the last minute to make his last arrangements. According to de Salmour he took "these religious precautions" in 1856, at a time when he was in his intellectual prime and the exercise of his will was still unrestricted. As far as his actual creed was concerned, one can trace from his youth, and especially from his first journey to Paris, the gradual emancipation of his thought. That dogmas soon ceased to concern him is evident; yet he continued to regard Christianity as the satisfaction of man's highest and most potent religious instincts, as an essential principle of civilisation for nations and of moral support for individuals. In short, he was an indulgent and sympathetic agnostic. This may be taken as the state of his religious feelings on the day when the Franciscan went to him in his room.

What passed between these two on the particular question of retraction? No one will ever know. But it is doubtful if Father Giacomo endeavoured to impose on his penitent a condition that he knew had been repelled beforehand. One can only think that if he tried it, it was unsuccessfully. In reality, Cavour had not committed in his own interests those sacrileges that gave rise to the terrible Bull of 25 March 1860, nor in a spirit of acquisitiveness, concupiscence, or ambition, as had Talleyrand. If Victor Emmanuel's minister had not flinched before the thunderbolts of the Vatican, it was because of one leading consideration: the high interests of the cause to which he had dedicated his life and his soul—the Italian cause. Upon this subject Cavour

would neither give way nor compromise, because his patriotic faith far surpassed his religious faith, because his
country was his true religion. Though it cost him life
everlasting, he could not retract. He calls to mind the
humble Jansenist who, called upon to subscribe to a doctrinal
compromise, said : " You threaten to deprive me of the Last
Sacrament if I do not bear witness to what I believe false. . . .
What does it matter to me if I die poor when treasure awaits
me in the grave ! "

Hardly had the dying man received the Viaticum, when
the King was announced. Cavour tried to raise himself
in the bed. " Ah ! Sire," he said, " the many things there
are to tell you, the many papers to show you ! . . . But I am
too ill." Yet he forced himself to speak of current affairs.
Victor Emmanuel, very cordial—for he was much moved
—stayed but a short time.

Left alone with his brother, his niece, and several friends,
Cavour continued seriously, as if all his work were passing
in review before him, as if he were reciting his *Nunc dimittis
servum tuum, Domine* : " Italy is almost finished. There are
neither Lombards, Piedmontese, Romagnese, nor Tuscans
any more ; we are all Italians. But there are still the Nea-
politans. Much corruption in their country ! It is not
their fault ; they have been governed so badly. They must
be educated now, taught virtue and liberty. Above all no
martial law, no martial law ! . . . Gallant Garibaldi, I bear
him no grudge. He wants to go to Rome and Venice ;
but so do I ! . . . It's another matter in Tyrol and Istria ;
that's for another generation. We have done enough, all
of us ; we have made Italy. *Si l'Italia è, la cosa va. . . .*"

Suddenly his strength failed; his voice could hardly be heard. His old servant, terrified, said in simple matter of fact : " M. le Comte's voice fails. When M. le Comte stops speaking, M. le Comte will die."

On 6 June, towards five o'clock in the morning, after having received Extreme Unction, he became icy-cold. But he was still quite conscious. A last sparkle showed in his eyes as he turned them on his niece. He kissed her twice. " Good-bye, and thank you, again, my dear little one ! " Then to Father Giacomo : " *Frate, frate, libera Chiesa in libero Stato !* " At a quarter to seven he died.

CONCLUSION

In the fine twelfth chapter of *Considérations sur la grandeur et la décadence des Romains*, Montesquieu, setting forth " the State of Rome after the death of Cæsar," invites the reader to think how advantageous it would be for the great actors on the world's stage, if they could " finish the part they were playing in the world at whatever period they wished." This, he says, is the explanation of the fact that so many illustrious Romans had recourse to suicide. Cavour loved life too well to leave it by his own act; it was life that left Cavour, without giving him sufficient time to consolidate his work. He died before the fifth act. Yet he had conceived and built up the whole play with so much vigour that it was enacted to the end as if the principal player were still in the leading part.

One year after his sudden death, the Comtesse de Circourt, a woman of fine intellect between whom and Cavour a rare attachment had existed, wrote to Nigra : " Thinking again upon the time that immediately followed that cruel blow, and comparing the situation in which it placed Italy with the present situation of affairs, one discovers that M. de Cavour's most extraordinary and final success is the work his *genius still carries on after his death.* This is the only measure by which the dimensions of his great and historic figure may be computed. The works of ordinary men do not endure even as long as they themselves endure ; a clever ingenuity brings them a momentary triumph; unfavourable circumstances work their ruin. Count de Cavour still directs the destiny of a country he miraculously called to political life. In the impetus given by his hand is his power preserved."

His successors in the work, Ricasoli, Rattazzi, Minghetti, La Marmora, prospered indeed only to the exact extent to which Cavour's programme and methods inspired them. Regarding Rome, the famous convention of 15 September 1864, that sounded the knell of Papal royalty throughout the world, was but an amplification of the engagements negotiated by Cavour, on the eve of his death, to effect the withdrawal of the French troops. In the case of Venice the parallel is not less striking. It was in 1866, on the morrow of Sadowa, that Italy with Prussia's co-operation obtained Venetia. As early as 1858 Cavour had declared: "The alliance of Italy and Prussia is written in letters of gold in the book of the history of the future." Two years later, at the time of Castelfidardo, he emphasised this conviction: "The independence of Italy and that of Germany are implicitly implied the one by the other, for they are the two corner-stones of the new European building." Here we see sketched the Prusso-Italian coalition of 8 April 1866— a coalition feverishly encouraged by Napoleon III by every means in his power, as if he feared the loss of Sedan!

Could Italy have been created without Cavour? It is as though one asked if the American Revolution could have been brought about without Washington. It becomes then a question of estimating the value of individual effort in the conduct of human affairs, the value of initiative, will-power, intellect, audacity, of one man's ability, at grips with the infinitely complex nature of the unknown forces that rule the world. It is no more than a paradox for Tolstoy to depict the great figures in history as puppets and tools, " having no influence upon the irresistible progress of events." On the other hand, has not Richelieu greatly exaggerated the efficacy of individual action, and is he not rather too regardless of the natural course of events when he declares in his trenchant way : " If they had imprisoned Luther whenever he began to preach, they would have had no Reformation " ?

It would of course be useless to pretend that Cavour was the sole creator of the *Risorgimento*. Preparing through long ages, hidden during centuries in the heart of the people, heralded by all thinkers and poets since Dante and Petrarch, the awakening of Italy was pre-eminently a manifestation of the national spirit. But in the *Risorgimento*, as it was brought about under Cavour's leadership, there was nothing that was inevitable or pre-ordained, either in the method or the time of its accomplishment. Far from it. If the organisation and direction of the *Risorgimento* had remained in the hands of the revolutionaries, the national drama would have degenerated into barren chaos. The end would not have come for twenty or thirty years, and then only after many futile revolts, after many risings and conspiracies had been suppressed with bloodshed. From the day on which Cavour took charge, everything changed both in internal and in external affairs. Italian patriotism was disciplined under the banner of Savoy ; a new spirit animated it ; dissension, disunion, vain dreaming, gave way to ordered, logical, and practical action. Thenceforward, decisive events followed upon one another in logical sequence as if one gave birth to another. Thus, the dispatch of an expeditionary corps to the Crimea led to participation in the Congress of Paris; to the interview at Plombières; to the Franco-Piedmontese Alliance of 28 January 1859; to Magenta and Solferino; to the Treaty of Zurich; to the annexation of the Duchies, of the Romagna, and of Tuscany; to the interview at Chambéry; to Castelfidardo; to Naples; to Palermo; and finally to the proclamation of the Kingdom of Italy. In this linked chain of events can we not see the guiding hand, the controlling mind?

An attempt to account for the special quality that enabled Cavour to obtain such results, discloses that it was the union in him of faculties generally incompatible if they are especially keen. Daring with prudence, for example; flexibleness with opinionativeness; impetuous driving power with charming persuasiveness; methodical calculation with intuitive anticipation; keen intellect with potent inspiration; vivid imagination with cold reason; an equal aptitude for comprehending general ideas or positive facts; material interests and the interests of the common weal. The union of these attributes made him at one and the same time the man for national crisis and the man for orderly government. In the supreme hierarchy of statesmen none transcends him.

FINIS

INDEX

INDEX